OPEN GOVERNMENT

The British Interpretation

RONALD WRAITH, C.B.E.

Senior Research Officer
Royal Institute of Public Administration

ROYAL INSTITUTE OF PUBLIC ADMINISTRATION

First published in 1977

Published by the Royal Institute of Public Administration, Hamilton House, Mabledon Place, London, WC1H 9BD.

Printed in England by Victoria House Publishing Co., 46–50 Sun Street, London EC2.

ISBN 0 900628 15 4

OPEN GOVERNMENT

The British Interpretation

RIPA RESEARCH BOOKLETS

THE MAJOR PUBLIC CORPORATIONS:
A STATUTORY ANALYSIS

David Peirson

FINANCING PUBLIC SECTOR PENSIONS

Raymond Nottage

APPRAISAL FOR STAFF DEVELOPMENT:
A PUBLIC SECTOR STUDY

Ronald Wraith

THE CONSUMER CAUSE:
A SHORT ACCOUNT OF ITS ORGANIZATION,
DEVELOPMENT, POWER AND IMPORTANCE

Ronald Wraith

FOREWORD

This is the fifth of a series of studies whose aim is to provide information and ideas on topical problems or recent developments of some importance in public administration and to do so, for the benefit of busy people, within the compass of a pamphlet rather than a book. It has the dual purpose of drawing together the threads of its subject, in order that discussion can start from a basis of fact, and of identifying its growing points and possible future direction.

The subject of 'Open Government' is highly topical and at the same time ill-defined. It is hoped that this essay may help to move discussion from the level of political slogan to that of serious practical consideration.

The Institute became interested in the subject some two years ago through an international seminar of the International Institute of Administrative Sciences in Brussels, initiated by Professor Donald Rowat of Carleton University, Ottawa, at which Mr. Wraith was the United Kingdom *rapporteur*. As a result of the U.K. Government's current interest in the subject, however, the paper which he subsequently contributed has become out of date—and indeed the present essay had to be revised at the last moment to take into account important Government pronouncements of November 1976.

The author has been greatly assisted, as authors writing for the RIPA publications are invariably assisted, by a number of busy people who have spared the time to check and comment on the draft. Chief among them are Mr. J. G. Pilling of the Home Office; Mr. B. H. Bliss, Legal Adviser to the Electricity Council, who helped with the passages on the nationalized industries; Mr. L. R. Roberts of the Association of County Councils, who did the same for local government; Mr. James Ascher of the American Embassy; and Mrs. Wanja Tornberg and Mr. Martin Rosen of the Swedish Embassy.

Any views expressed are the author's own and do not necessarily commit the Institute or those who helped him.

The Royal Institute of Public Administration
January 1977

CONTENTS

INTRODUCTION

This essay discusses what has come to be called 'open government', a fashionable expression whose general intention is reasonably clear but whose practical meaning awaits clarification.

In general terms it is about the public's right of access to official information, a subject in which the practice of governments stems from one of two premises—the first, that such information should be freely available except where specific reasons can be adduced for its restriction; the second, that the public have no such right of access unless it can be shown that it would be in the public interest to allow it. In actual practice the gap between the two may not be as great as is commonly supposed; in the mental attitudes engendered by the respective assumptions, and the spirit in which government is conducted as a result, it is perhaps a good deal wider.

Open government lends itself to easy generalizations of this kind and the phrase has acquired a challenging democratic ring. What it may mean in practice is somewhat obscure, since this must turn on points of puzzling detail—for example what is a 'working paper', when does a policy-forming file become a policy document, to what extent may civil servants keep private memoranda? These questions have been fairly clearly, though by no means exactly, determined in Sweden and are in the process of clarification in the United States—these being the countries where open government is held by its advocates to have become most highly developed. They are discussed in Chapter 3.

An aspect of the subject of particular importance in Great Britain is the Official Secrets Acts, especially section 2 of the Official Secrets Act 1911. Official secrets should in theory be a comparatively minor aspect of the subject of open government, which ought to have positive rather than negative connotations. In Britain it occupies a place of disproportionate importance largely because this country has inherited an Official Secrets Act (that of 1911) whose passing by Parliament was rooted in misunderstanding and whose existence in the late twentieth century is now generally considered to be anomalous. It has been applied, on the whole, with moderation and good sense, but this cannot remove its two fundamental flaws—first, that its invocation (by the Government) is uncertain and therefore, in the strict sense of the word, arbitrary; and second, that its meaning is obscure. The abolition or amendment of the Act has occupied the attention of British governments since 1971, and is proving particularly troublesome to the Government at the time of writing.

In 1968 the Fulton Report on the Future of the Civil Service suggested that 'the administrative process was surrounded by too much secrecy' and that 'the public interest would be better served if there were a greater amount of openness'. The Report proposed that the Government should set up an investigation into the matter, and that among other things 'the Official Secrets Acts would need to be included in such a review'.

This investigation was duly carried out by the Labour Government of the day 'on a wide inter-departmental basis' and resulted in a White Paper 'Information and the Public Interest' (Cmnd. 4089) which is referred to more fully below (p. 21).

The Conservative Government which succeeded to office in 1970 had undertaken in its Party Manifesto to eliminate unnecessary secrecy concerning the working of government and to review the operation of the Official Secrets Act, in fulfilment of which they appointed a Home Office Departmental Committee headed by Lord Franks. But although the Manifesto had been expressed in broad and general terms, the terms of reference of the Committee were narrow and specific—to investigate the 'operation of Section 2 of the Official Secrets Act 1911'. The Committee reported, with recommendations, in September 1972.[1] As will be seen from the footnote, the Franks Report, as it is commonly called, is the equivalent of a book of 1,300 pages, and it is improbable that any facet of the subject escaped the Committee's attention. This essay naturally draws on it considerably, and an attempt is made later to assess the Report and its probable outcome.

The Franks Report was debated in the House of Commons in June 1973[2] (see p. 62 *infra*), since when there has been a change of government. It is not, however, a subject on which the major political parties differ very much, though neither appears to find it straightforward; nor, of course, will it be easy to find parliamentary time for such legislation. The Queen's Speech on 19 November 1975 included the following:

'Proposals will be prepared to amend the Official Secrets Act 1911 and to liberalize the practices relating to official information.'

The wording is important for two reasons. First, it makes clear that the Government were concerned not only with the negative aspect of the subject (official secrets) but with the positive one (open government). Second, the Government pledged themselves to 'prepare proposals', not

---

[1] Report of Departmental Committee on Section 2 of the Official Secrets Act 1911, Cmnd. 5104, pp. 144, Vol. 2 Written Evidence, pp. 423. Vol. 3 Oral Evidence mainly from Government witnesses pp. 369. Vol. 4 Oral Evidence mainly from Non-Government witnesses pp. 413.

[2] H.C. Deb., 29 June 1973, Vol. 858, cols. 1885–1973.

to introduce a Bill, suggesting that legislation was probably low in their order of priorities.

In view of their other preoccupations it remains low, and it is now known that there is no possibility of legislation before the 1977–8 Session of Parliament. However, the undertaking given in the Queen's Speech has been honoured in that a Cabinet committee—according to press reports—of senior ministers and civil servants has had the Franks proposals under review since 1975 and by chance a certain urgency was injected into the Government's consideration of the matter by the publication of Cabinet discussions on social security benefits in *New Society* in 1976. The Committee's proposals, we may assume, formed the basis of a statement of intent by the Home Secretary on 22 November 1976[3] which is summarized—in the section commenting on the Franks Report—in the concluding chapter.

The *New Society* affair led directly to the appointment of a Committee of Privy Councillors under the chairmanship of Lord Houghton 'to examine the procedures for handling Cabinet and Cabinet committee papers inside the Government . . .' and the Report of this Committee[4] is also mentioned in the concluding chapter.

The Cabinet Committee and the Houghton Committee were dealing with issues of a quite different order, a point worth emphasizing since some press reports at the time did not appear to appreciate that there was any distinction.

It is proposed, first, to set out the contentious provisions of the Official Secrets Act 1911 and to distinguish between what the Act says and what happens in practice; second, to indicate the liberalizing trends, discernible throughout the 1960s, in the direction of more open government generally; and third, to consider whether there are in fact substantial differences between the 'closed' system of the U.K. and the 'open' systems elsewhere, of which Sweden and the U.S.A. are commonly quoted as the outstanding examples.

We shall then examine the responsibilities which currently rest on public servants to give or to withhold information; the extent to which their work may be subject to investigation, thus limiting the extent to which it can in any case be regarded as 'secret'; and the problem of official secrecy as it affects the press.

Finally, as we have said, we shall try to assess the Franks Report and its possible outcome. If this booklet serves no other purpose it will be justified as a reminder of this important document, of which too little is known at a time when official secrecy is being widely, and on the whole

[3] H.C. Deb., 22 November 1976, Vol. 919, c. 1878–88.
[4] Published by HMSO on 30 November 1976.

sensationally, publicized.

So far as *receiving* information is concerned (in the knowledge that it is being improperly communicated) the Official Secrets Acts naturally apply to every citizen in the land. But those who are in a position to *give* such information are bound by them in a particular way—that is to say they may be required to sign a declaration that they are aware of the provisions of the Acts and the consequences of breaching them.

Although government departments are the main repositories of official information, especially of the more 'sensitive' kind, and although it is primarily civil servants who are bound in this particular way, important information of a comparable kind is also held by nationalized industries, where the special application of the Acts is rather more complicated, and by local authorities, where it does not prevail at all. Some account is therefore given of their position at appropriate points in the essay.

THE OFFICIAL SECRETS ACT 1911

The first Official Secrets Act of 1889 was replaced by that of 1911. This was amended in 1920 and 1939, but the legislation has not been consolidated. Hence the occasional use in this essay of the phrase 'Official Secrets Acts' in the plural; the principal references, however, are to the Act of 1911.

Section 1 of the 1911 Act is concerned with spying, and is uncontroversial. The contentious part of the Act is section 2, which reads as follows:

Text of section 2 of the 1911 Act (as amended)
'Wrongful communication etc. of information

(1) if any person having in his possession or control any secret official code word, or pass word, or any sketch, plan, model, article, note, document, or information which relates to or is used in a prohibited place or anything in such a place or which has been made or obtained in contravention of this Act, or which has been entrusted in confidence to him by any person holding office under Her Majesty or which he has obtained or to which he has had access owing to his position as a person who holds or has held office under Her Majesty, or as a person who holds or has held a contract made on behalf of Her Majesty or as a person who is or has been employed under a person who holds or has held such an office or contract

(*a*) communicates the code word, pass word, sketch, plan, model, note, document, or information to any person, other than a person to whom he is authorised to communicate it, or a person to whom it is in the interest of the State his duty to communicate it; or

(*aa*) uses the information in his possession for the benefit of any foreign Power or in any other manner prejudicial to the safety or interests of the State;

(*b*) retains the sketch, plan, model, article, note, or document in his possession or control when he has no right to retain it or when it is contrary to his duty to retain it, or fails to comply with all directions issued by lawful authority with regard to the return or disposal thereof; or

(*c*) fails to take reasonable care of, or so conducts himself as to endanger the safety of the sketch, plan, model, article, note,

13

document, secret official code or pass word or information; that person shall be guilty of a misdemeanour.

(1A) If any person having in his possession or control any sketch, plan, model, article, note, document, or information which relates to munitions of war, communicates it directly or indirectly to any foreign Power, or in any other manner prejudicial to the safety or interests of the State, that person shall be guilty of a misdemeanour.

(2) If any person receives any secret official code word, or pass word, or sketch, plan, model, article, note, document, or information, knowing or having reasonable ground to believe, at the time when he receives it, that the code word, pass word, sketch, plan, model, article, note, document, or information is communicated to him in contravention of this Act, he shall be guilty of a misdemeanour, unless he proves that the communication to him of the code word, pass word, sketch, plan, model, article, note, document, or information was contrary to his desire.'

We discuss, first, how the Act came to be passed and second, what section 2 means.

The circumstances in which Parliament approved the Bill were unusual and, it now appears, somewhat discreditable. It was introduced into the Lords in the July of a year when there was national anxiety about German espionage, with which it purported to deal, and for which the 1889 Act had proved inadequate. The Lords spent perhaps half an hour on it on the Second Reading debate (H.L. Deb., 25 July 1911). It was introduced by the Secretary of State for War and two other lords spoke briefly. The remarks of all three were confined to the presence of strange figures seen in fortifications and dockyards, behaving suspiciously and suspected of sketching or photographing. The Bill was sent to the House of Commons on 2 August and passed through all its stages in one day (H.C. Deb., 18 August 1911). It was introduced by the Under Secretary of State for War and went through the Committee stage without amendment, though the House divided 107–10.[1] Section 2, the cause of our present discontents, was not once mentioned either in the Lords or the Commons.

The Franks Report says forthrightly that 'Parliament was not given full explanations of the 1911 Bill, and did not examine it in detail'. An idea has been created that it was an emergency measure dealing with a crisis in national security, and that the intention of section 2 was to be a

---

[1] Five of the ten were Keir Hardie, Arthur Henderson, George Lansbury, Ramsay Macdonald and Philip Snowden.

kind of backstop to section 1, which specifically deals with espionage. The Franks Committee's research into the official files disclosed that this does not represent the facts. It is true that the 1889 Act had proved to be inadequate, but not only for dealing with the Queen's enemies. Leakages, and publication of other official information, comparable to those which cause concern in our own day, had continued between 1889 and 1911, and section 2, aimed at preventing this, had been long in preparation; there had in fact been unsuccessful attempts to introduce amending legislation in 1896 and 1908. An impression survives that section 2 was drafted in a hurry and must not be taken to mean literally what it says. According to Franks it was drafted with great care and was intended to mean precisely what it says; but the fact was not mentioned to Parliament by government spokesmen.

So it was that Parliament, believing that it was plugging a hole in our national defences by clamping down on German spies, before going off for a deferred summer vacation, placed the threat of criminal sanctions on every Crown servant and every reporter for the unauthorized disclosure of—for example in the 1970s—plans to curtail the railway network or the Cabinet's views on paying children's allowances to wives instead of husbands, two subjects which the Parliament of 1911 would have had difficulty in comprehending. So it was that the unauthorized disclosure of *any* information, by *any* Crown servant or its reception by *any* person who knew it to be unauthorized, was brought within the purview of the criminal law.

It is this 'blanket' nature of section 2 which causes it to be criticized. There are no qualifications, no degrees, no discriminations. Its tentacles are all-embracing. It can be made to appear ridiculous by saying (as is true) that if a civil servant tells his wife over supper what he has been doing during the day he is committing a criminal offence. More realistic but only slightly less absurd examples could be imagined, and it is said that the Act is breached almost every hour of the day when Crown servants talk to each other or to their friends and acquaintances.

The facts, in real life, are somewhat less sensational, since it is the *unauthorized* communication of information that is an offence, and the concept of authorization, though elusive, is sufficiently elastic. That it is by no means a *simple* concept was apparent from the evidence given by civil servants to the Franks Committee, this being one of the matters in public adminsitration that are as dependent on convention as on rule. But generally speaking civil servants know instinctively, and from experience, what they should communicate, and to whom; many will be doing work in which the need to communicate is implicit, a few where it is quite explicit; most will rely on common sense, reinforced by the knowledge that disciplinary measures, or a black mark against their promotion prospects, may result from being too communicative.

Accordingly the Official Secrets Act does not *of itself* prevent the flow of information to the public or the press.

Nor has section 2 been used in an oppressive manner. Not only has good sense restricted its application but a prosecution under its terms requires the personal authorization of the Attorney-General. Between 1945 and 1971 there was no more than 23 prosecutions, and of these at least 17 concerned ordinary criminal activities about which no critic of the Act would be likely to cavil—i.e. 10 were security or defence leaks, five were plots to promote theft (or in one case abortion) and two concerned the sale of documents for profit. Thirty-four defendants were involved in all, of whom 27 were convicted and six acquitted. Two-thirds were civil servants or former civil servants; two were journalists.

On the other hand, four of the six acquittals were in a single case—the notorious case of the *Sunday Telegraph* and the Nigerian civil war in 1971, mentioned more fully on page 52, and in this instance the judge made no secret of his hostility to section 2 of the Act. We may suppose that the Act no longer reflects enlightened opinion on the safeguarding of necessary secrecy, since the judge's opinion is shared by many responsible bodies representing the legal profession, the press and public opinion generally. But the fact that prosecutions have averaged less than one a year, and that most of these concerned military security or ordinary crime, suggests that section 2 has not been used unreasonably.

Nevertheless, although the more sweeping condemnations of section 2 may be largely discounted, it remains an objectionable measure. Two of the objections bear particularly hardly on the press. The first is its indiscriminate nature, whereby treason and corruption on the one hand, and the reporting of domestic information which a journalist might think was of public interest on the other, are lumped together as if they were crimes of the same order; it is not surprising that the press should find this repugnant. The other is its uncertainty, whereby an editor may not know whether the disclosure of what he wishes to publish will be held to be criminal or not. He must guess whether the Attorney-General will authorize prosecution or take the risk that he will not. It is not impossible (instances are given in the evidence to Franks) for section 2 to be held over the press as a threat.

Again, it seems questionable whether it should be a criminal offence for a man to *receive* information, even if he makes no use of it. Admittedly there is a proviso that he must have known that it was being improperly communicated, and he is cleansed of guilt if it can be shown that he read or listened to the illicit information 'contrary to his desire'. But it

16

would seem more equitable to say that those who have secrets should keep them, and if they fail to do so they and they alone should suffer the penalty.

It is, however, probable that the ill effects of the section are indirect and subtle rather than specific—that it has helped to create the atmosphere of secrecy which the Fulton Committee deplored, and has made civil servants, discreet by nature, unduly cautious in disclosing information. This is not to suggest that they live under the shadow of the Act or consciously ponder whether they are observing it—on the contrary most of them probably never give it a thought after the first few years of their career. But every civil servant signs a declaration, couched in somewhat forbidding terms, at the beginning of his career (and on retirement) that his attention has been drawn to the terms of the Official Secrets Acts and that he understands the consequences of not abiding by them.[2] Subconsciously, if not consciously, this may engender an attitude of mind whereby the citizen in search of information is expected to prove that he ought to have it, rather than that the civil servant should prove that he ought *not* to have it, which is perhaps the essential difference between 'closed' and 'open' systems of government.

---

[2] The Franks Report (paras. 35 and 36) maintains that the terms in which these declarations are written are both confusing and misleading, especially on the meaning of authorization.

LIBERALIZING TRENDS

Whatever inhibiting effects the Official Secrets Acts may have had, they have not prevented a number of developments—notably in the 1960s—which have greatly extended public knowledge of matters which were previously confidential. These developments support our previous statement that official secrets are a comparatively incidental aspect of open government, since a liberalizing trend, unaffected by the Acts, has been fostered by administrative decision, legislation and court judgements alike.

The clearest example of access to official documents being extended by *administrative decision* was the release in 1962 to the parties concerned of inspectors' reports to the minister on their findings and recommendations regarding planning inquiries. Until then these reports were not available outside the Ministry, so that the loser of a case did not know why he had lost or what the inspector said. The decision to publish them was not, it must be admitted, taken at all willingly. Indeed, the fight of the civil servants concerned against publication is worth study today. It is recorded in the Minutes of Evidence to the Committee on Administrative Tribunals and Enquiries (curiously enough, also conducted under the chairmanship of Lord Franks)[1]. The Ministry of Housing and Local Government representatives were emphatic that publication would cause embarrassment, would be a hindrance to sound policy making and would create administrative difficulties amounting almost to chaos. In the event none of these gloomy prophecies was fulfilled and the atmosphere surrounding planning appeals became much healthier. Twenty years on, the Ministry's arguments illustrate the very obscurantism that Lord Fulton was to criticize in 1968. What is more to the point, Lord Franks's later report, on Section 2 of the Official Secrets Act, has much the same thing to say, for it is a recurring theme that much of what would be achieved by a change in the law relating to official secrets could equally well be achieved by a change in administrative discretion, and that the prime need is—still—a shift in mental attitudes.

Nevertheless, the publication of inspectors' reports was a pioneer step. However unwilling, the MHLG team was loyal to authority, and when the Report of the Committee on Administrative Tribunals and Enquiries

[1] Cmd. 218, July 1957. See especially Chapter 23 and Minutes of Evidence pp. 7, et seq.

said the reports ought to be published they straightway decided to publish them. And the very fact that their arguments remain on record for anyone to read, possibly causing them to be somewhat red in the face after 20 years, is itself a good advertisement for open government.

In 1967 the creation by *statute* of the office of Parliamentary Commissioner for Administration has meant that, provided a citizen could establish a *prima facie* grievance on grounds of maladministration, records and files would be disclosed that would previously have been inaccessible and the Commissioner's findings upon them published. This is admittedly a negative provision, in that it deals only with error and not with policy. Nevertheless it represents a large erosion of official secrecy.

In 1968 an important ruling by *the courts* modified the doctrine of Crown privilege, whereby, on the sole authority of a minister, official information could be withheld, on the ground that its disclosure would not be in the public interest, even though its discovery was important for the defence.[2] The House of Lords held that:

> 'The court has jurisdiction to order the disclosure of documents for which Crown privilege is claimed, as it is the right and duty of the court to hold the balance between the interests of the public in ensuring the proper administration of justice and the public interest in the withholding of documents whose disclosures would be contrary to the national interest.'

The Court went on to say, in effect, that due weight would be given to a minister's view, and that if the considerations were of a kind that judicial experience was not competent to weigh, the minister's view would prevail; but that it would be for the courts to decide whether disclosure should be made. This was a judgement of great importance to the subject under discussion.

Nevertheless, although these developments have enlarged public access to official information, the changing climate of opinion, and the trend towards more open government, are perhaps better exemplified by *political* decisions to publish government intentions, and to invite public comment on matters which the Government must shortly decide.

Consultative Documents

This trend has been especially discernible since about 1967, when the Government of the day introduced the 'Green Paper'. 'White Papers', in

---

[2] *Conway v. Rimmer* (1967) 2 All E.R. p. 1260 (Appeal Court).
(1968) 1 All E.R. p. 874 (House of Lords).

general, summarize the Government's conclusions on a particular matter, and their intentions about prospective legislation; although there is still a margin for amendment in the light of professional or parliamentary criticism, the main conclusions will stand. The Green Paper was novel in that it did not represent settled government policy, but was intended to set out the nature of a problem and the possible ways of dealing with it, and to invite public discussion which would be helpful to the Government when they came to bring the matter to a conclusion. Green Papers, and other kinds of consultative document, are now common, averaging as many as ten a year. They vary a good deal in character; some represent the Government's earliest stage of thinking, all of which is open to revision in the light of public reaction; others are obviously addressed, because of their subject matter, to small expert audiences rather than to the public at large; and some are biased towards imparting information as much as inviting discussion. But they have in common that they are about matters on which the Government have as yet reached no firm conclusion and on which they seek public reaction. Of the many Green Papers published since 1967 the first concerned a tentative proposal for a regional employment premium in development areas; among the most important which followed were two on the future of the national health service; others have been concerned with such disparate matters as the speed limit on the roads, value-added tax, the future shape of local government and the future of Northern Ireland.

Two consultative documents of great importance were published in March and April 1976. The first—*Transport Policy*—reviews the objectives of policy with regard to road and rail, and to the economy and the environment, discussing the various options that are open and the consequences of each. The second—*Priorities for Health and Personal Social Services in England*—breaks new ground in seeking public participation in an effort to 'establish rational and systematic priorities' throughout two related government services; at the time of writing it is the subject of very wide and open consultation. Thus two of the most pressing social problems of our time are open to public debate with a ministerial promise of readiness (to quote the then Secretary of State for Social Services) 'to modify strategic plans in the light of views expressed'.

The influence which Green Papers and other consultative documents may actually have had on the formation of policy is an attractive subject for research, which may well be in progress already. If so it is a growing field, for in the Debate on the Queen's Speech the Prime Minister foreshadowed a further 'liberalizing trend'.[3]

[3] H.C. Deb., Vol. 919, c. 24 November 1976.

He stated the Government's intention to double the number of Green Papers and other consultative documents to be released annually and said that they would include hitherto unpublished material drawn, for example, from Programme Analyses and Reviews (PARS) one of which, as is mentioned on page 44, had even been withheld only a few months earlier by the Department of Education and Science from a sub-committee of the Expenditure Committee.

In his speech the Prime Minister referred to a subject too little considered by the enthusiasts for open government—its *cost*—which he called 'the primary restraint on disclosure'. A substantial PAR could cost about £100,000 in its present internal form, a sum which publication would greatly increase; and the cost of the Swedish and American systems was one of the reasons for their rejection by the Cabinet Committee.

'Information and the Public Interest'

In 1969 the Government brought together the threads of our subject in a White Paper entitled 'Information and the Public Interest' (Cmnd. 4089), which was in effect the report of an internal inquiry recommended by the Fulton Committee into ways of getting rid of unnecessary secrecy. Though a somewhat self-congratulatory document, designed to show that the Government of the day was alive to the Fulton Committee's concern, the Report did confirm and document trends towards the increasing publication both of factual information, especially by the Government Central Statistical Office, and of forecasts upon which Government policy was being based, notably economic forecasts in relation to the budget. It also reported that civil servants were more and more emerging from anonymity, appearing on public occasions and giving interviews to the press, radio and television.

There were two pronouncements of a more general kind. First, the Government confirmed their belief in the value of secrecy at the actual policy-making stage, saying that civil servants and ministers alike should be able to discuss and disagree among themselves without feeling that their individual views could become a matter of public knowledge.

Second, they advanced the view, which was not well received in all quarters, that the Official Secrets Acts were 'not in any way a barrier to greater openness in government', since they related only to *unauthorized* disclosure, and the areas of authorization could always be extended. The tone, as much as the content, of this pronouncement offended those who did not accept that the Government alone should be the arbiter of what it was good for people to know; and the statement paid too little heed to the indirect, and frustrating, effects of the legislation.

Television and the Tape Recorder

These liberalizing trends within the administration, which have represented a slow and cautious approach to more open government, have been taking place against the background of a rapid and spectacular growth of a different kind of official 'openness'—on radio and television. This is not central to the subject of this essay but is sufficiently close to it to justify a brief digression.

Government policies are now ventilated to the public as never before, and even the process of policy formation has been presented on the television screen, with ministers and civil servants acting roles in a realistic situation. Ministers (and heads of nationalized industries) are constantly subjected to intense public questioning both on hour-long feature programmes and at impromptu interviews on every kind of occasion and always seem willing to meet the media's demands, while back-benchers who establish themselves as radio or television personalities have arguably more influence, and stimulate more interest in the large questions of the day, than many members of the Government. Whether this is to the advantage of democracy is perhaps an open question, but one argument for open government of a more formal and systematic kind is that it would moderate the influence of the professional communicator or popular personality and allow the work of Government and of the civil service to speak for itself.

*

To revert, the background of the subject so far as central government is concerned is that there is no acceptance of a general principle that the public have the right of access to official information; but that by a series of pragmatic arrangements such information is in fact quite widely available for particular purposes.

The position in local government differs in two ways. First, the provisions of the Official Secrets Act do not apply to the kind of information that is held by local authorities and there is no general requirement for either members or employees of local authorities to acknowledge their existence. Local authorities have the power, delegated to them by Parliament, of making their own Standing Orders which could, if desired, include rules about the unauthorized disclosure of information; indeed, Model Standing Orders suggested some years ago by the then Ministry of Housing and Local Government touch on the subject (see p. 40) but there is no evidence that local authorities as a whole regard official secrecy as an important feature of Standing Orders and the Ministry's own ideas have since been overtaken by new thinking on the subject. Second, local authorities—unlike government departments—have statutory obligations to provide public access to certain specified kinds of information.

'OPEN' AND 'CLOSED' SYSTEMS OF GOVERNMENT

An 'open' system of government is usually taken to mean one in which there is a positive requirement, either in the Constitution or in statutes, that Government shall disclose and give access to all official documents which have progressed beyond a certain stage, variously defined but conveniently summarized in the expression 'working papers', i.e. documents which represent firm decisions; with specified exceptions of matters which would harm the public interest if disclosed. A 'closed' system, by contrast, is one in which there is no such requirement but where it lies in the Government's discretion to make available official information which in their judgement it would be in the public interest to disclose.

In Sweden the general right of public access is enshrined in the Freedom of the Press Act 1949, an entrenched law which forms part of the Swedish Constitution and which is the successor to a comparable Act of 1812; in the U.S.A. it is enshrined in the Freedom of Information Act 1967 as amended in 1974. There is no comparable provision in Great Britain. On the other hand a direct comparison of this kind—as between any country and another—may be unprofitable without reference to the constitutional and conventional differences between the countries concerned. Both Sweden and the United States have written constitutions and each, in a different manner, practises a separation of powers between the legislature and the executive of a kind unfamiliar in Britain, where ministers are responsible for the execution of policy and accountable for it to Parliament. In Sweden the execution of policy is the function of autonomous boards, responsible neither to a minister nor to Parliament. Equally in the U.S. the doctrine of ministerial responsibility and accountability is unknown. These considerations, in the words of the Franks Report, determine 'both the degree of openness in government and the role and behaviour of the civil service'.

Indeed the Report repeatedly makes the point that political and constitutional factors have greater importance and relevance to openness in government than has legal provision, and although we question (p. 67) whether this is as true as it once was for Great Britain, it is clearly a factor to be borne in mind.

The points of interest in the context of this essay are firstly, the exceptions that are made in the interests of good government, i.e. the matters which still remain secret despite a general national commitment to openness; and second, how the law actually operates in practice at the level of the working administrator.

Matters Which Remain Secret in 'Open' Systems

In Sweden the constitutional requirement of public access to *all* official documents is subject (in the words of the Freedom of the Press Act, Chapter 2, Article 1):

' . . . only to such restrictions as are demanded either out of consideration for the security of the Realm and its relations with foreign powers, or with regard to the activities for inspection, control or other supervision carried out by public authorities, or for the prevention and prosecution of crime, or in order to protect the legitimate economic interests of the State, communities and individuals, or out of consideration for the maintenance of privacy, security of the person, decency and morality.'

The Act goes on to state that those cases in which official documents, in accordance with these principles, are to be kept secret shall be clearly defined in a specific act of law, and the Act in which they are so defined is the Secrecy Act 1937, a non-constitutional Act, that is to say one which can be amended in the ordinary way.

In the United States the documents which must be made available 'for public inspection and copying' are defined in the Freedom of Information Act as:

final opinions, including concurring and dissenting opinions, as well as orders, made in the adjudication of cases

those statements of policy and interpretations which have been adopted by the agency and are not published in the Federal Register and

administrative staff manuals and instructions to staff that affect a member of the public'

Documents which may be classified as confidential and withheld from public inspection are (in somewhat summarized form) those which concern:

Secret national security or foreign policy information
(Varous statutes, notably the Espionage Act, protect specific kinds of information in this field)

Internal personnel practices

Information exempted by law (e.g. income tax returns)

Trade secrets or other confidential, commercial or financial information

Privileged inter-agency or intra-agency memoranda

Personal information, personnel or medical files

Law enforcement investigatory information

Information relating to reports on financial institutions

Geological and geophysical information.

It will be seen that there is a good deal in common in the reserved matters in the two countries, as presumably there must be in all countries whose system of government is nearer the 'open' than the 'closed' end of the spectrum.

On the other hand there is one important matter in which the two countries differ, namely individual privacy. In spite of the declaration in the Swedish Constitutional Act about the 'maintenance of privacy' the Secrecy Act does not provide adequate safeguards and it is not impossible for members of the public to obtain access to private information about other individuals. In the United States, on the other hand, individual privacy is safeguarded not only in the general provisions of the Freedom of Information Act itself but in a subsequent Privacy Act of 1975, in conjunction with which the Freedom of Information Act has now to be interpreted.

Another difference is that in Sweden Cabinet records are closed for varying periods of time and among specified documents that may remain secret are those concerned with labour relations and wage negotiations.

Openness in government, in terms of what the public may know for the asking, is accordingly a relative matter, and the gap between Sweden and the United States on the one hand and the United Kingdom on the other is narrower than might be supposed. This is to some extent borne out by the actual prosecutions made under section 2 of the British Official Secrets Act since 1945. Of the 22 cases (out of 23) which actually came to trial (see p. 16) 19 could have been *prima facie* criminal offences in Sweden and the United States; of the other three, two were criminal charges but the defendants were acquitted.[1]

---

[1] The remaining case was that of the *Sunday Telegraph* and the Nigerian civil war (p. 52).

Practical Operation

On the other hand, in those large areas of administration where access is *not* restricted in Sweden and the United States the public's rights are, to British eyes, remarkable. They may see on demand, and indeed copy and publish, documents which in Whitehall would be invisible for thirty years.

In Sweden, for example, the public can read a minister's incoming and outgoing mail if it has not been classified as confidential by a responsible official. To be accurate, the concept of classification does not apply in Sweden except to a limited number of documents 'the secrecy of which is of eminent importance for the security of the Realm' (Constitutional Act, Chapter 2, Article 14). What happens is that officials use their own discretion in interpreting the Secrecy Act to withhold or release documents, but there is an automatic safeguard against over-caution on their part since an applicant who is refused information may appeal to the minister, the ombudsman or in certain cases to the courts, and unwarranted refusal by a public servant would be considered reprehensible.

The public are able to identify the documents they wish to see from a register of letters, memoranda, policy papers etc., briefly described, which is on public access and kept up-to-date daily or twice weekly.

As we have said, 'working papers' may be withheld, but they are not always easy to define with precision and again officials are wise to err on the side of liberality rather than caution because of the possibility of appeal. Actually this is somewhat surprising, since Articles 4 and 5 of the Constitutional Act do appear to be reasonably precise and to leave officials plenty of discretion to withhold papers which relate only to the provisional stages of a decision, e.g.:

'A memorandum or other note prepared or drawn up by an authority solely to present a case or matter or to prepare it for decision shall not be deemed to be an official document in the hands of such authority unless, after the case or matter has been finally settled by the authority, the note has been taken in charge for the purpose of being kept.' (Art. 4)

'Minutes and other similar records shall be deemed to be drawn up when they have been revised and approved by the authority or when they have otherwise been made ready. Other documents relating to a particular case or matter shall be deemed to be prepared when they have been despatched, or if they are not despatched, when the case or matter has been finally settled by the authority.' (Art. 5)

Nevertheless in actual practice officials are never quite certain that *any* memorandum, diary or journal may not be judged public property. This may have the possibly undesirable effect, in matters of delicacy or difficulty, of encouraging telephone conversations and rough personal notes rather than formal letters or minutes which would manifestly have to go on file.

If it is clear that documents are *not* confidential they must be made available promptly and photocopies (to be paid for by the applicant) provided on request. They may include such items as ordinary mail (over 80 per cent of incoming and outgoing prime ministerial mail is on public record), minutes of internal meetings, civil servants' expense accounts, even personal diaries. Such regulations apply to State and municipal agencies alike.

It is not easy to say to what extent 'the public' take advantage of their opportunities, since the amount of information that is reserved (and for that matter the amount that is at all interesting in any popular sense) must vary from one ministry to another. A high proportion of documents in the Foreign Affairs and Defence Ministries is secret in any case; on the other hand the Ministry of Justice contains much that is newsworthy as well as of professional interest to lawyers and the Prime Minister's Office deals with a wide variety of affairs. But it is the agencies dealing with social security, planning and municipal affairs that are most regularly used, primarily by the press, whose reporters keep the registers under close observation, to a lesser extent by individual members of the public.

It must be recalled by British readers, who may have a mental picture of Whitehall departments besieged by crowds hungry to read their mail, that the population of Sweden is little more than eight million and that of Stockholm about 750,000. Although the Swedish press and public take regular advantage of the Freedom of the Press Act its administration does not prove unduly burdensome.

In the United States the Freedom of Information Act of 1967, though admirable in conception, was largely evaded in practice by various forms of 'foot-dragging' and passive resistance. Unlike Swedish practice the release of a document was a matter for the agency and not for the individual who originated it, and this gave scope for slow procedures and unwarranted delays. There were also costly fees, unreasonable requirements for the precise identification of documents and, not least, over-classification. Nor were the public sufficiently aware of their rights. The amending Act of 1974, passed by Congress over Presidential veto, sought to remedy these shortcomings; in the stately words of the Washington Information Directory 1975–6 it 'removes some of the obstacles which the bureaucracy had erected since 1967'.

The Act does not amend the substance of its predecessor but it lays down first, wide-ranging requirements for publicity and ease of access to individual agency information officers and second, stringent procedural rules for the processing of requests for information.

All agencies of the executive branch are required to publish in the Federal Register details of their record systems and to appoint officers whose business it is to implement the provisions of the Act and to assist the public in the exercise of their rights under it. Strict identification of documents has been abandoned in favour of a 'reasonable description' of what is wanted. There is to be a uniform scale of fees for searching and copying and strict time limits for responses to requests—ten working days for an initial request, twenty for an appeal from an initial refusal to produce documents and thirty for an agency to respond to a complaint filed in court under the terms of the Act. Such cases are to be given priority over all other business before the courts, both at first instance and on appeal, and federal district courts are empowered to order agencies to produce the contested material and to determine *in camera* whether it was properly exempted. Finally, each agency is required to make an annual report to Congress, including a list of all decisions to withhold information requested under the Act; the reasons, the appeals and the results; all relevant rules; the fee schedule; and the names of officials responsible for each denial of information.

The effect of these comprehensive requirements has been to create a new Freedom of Information secretariat in every agency of government and great demands are being made on their staffs. Even in the short time since the Act became effective (February 1975) a flood of information has been released, not least by the State Department and the FBI, of a kind that would have been thought impossible a few years ago.

The kind of document which may be legitimately withheld by virtue of being a 'working paper' or its equivalent awaits precise definition, which will no doubt emerge gradually as case law is built up by the district courts. Meanwhile, as in Sweden, officials are disposed to err on the side of liberality, and hesitate to withhold anything (unless it is clearly classifiable) beyond the most personal *aide-memoires*.

Unlike Sweden, where the press are prominent among those seeking information, most of the demands in these early days have come from lawyers, interest groups, trade unions and private individuals, including scholars and researchers.

One of the most serious abuses—if that is not too strong a term—during the pre-1974 period was over-classification. A recent State Department instruction has this to say:

'We have in the past either classified unnecessarily, classified too highly, or held classified too long, the bulk of our records . . . we still tend to over-classify and are too little concerned with timely de-classification.'

All federal agencies are now under instruction to limit classication to the essential minimum and to place on each classified document a pro-visional date for de-classification.

To sum up, the 1974 Act provided the teeth that were lacking in its predecessor. It has been widely acclaimed by the public, viewed with some concern by the older generation of administrators and generated an enormous amount of activity. No one has yet calculated the cost.

The Position in the United Kingdom

With Swedish and American practice in mind, it is instructive to read the evidence to the Franks Committee of the press in its various repre-sentative forms, and to see whether they complain that information is withheld in the United Kingdom that is not withheld elsewhere. What emerges is not so much a list of specific complaints (though these exist) as a more generalized complaint about uncertainty, which can take various forms. Even in defence matters some civil servants will—it is said—disclose more than others, or will disclose more to people they know than to others; information is often available in scattered pub-lished sources, including overseas sources, which can be brought to-gether by an investigating journalist in a way which could bring him under the shadow of the Official Secrets Act, even though he had con-travened no law in putting it together; again, the Act can be used as a threat, or indeed as a bluff, when what is at stake is not so much the national interest as administrative inconvenience or embarrassment.

The real gulf between the open systems and the British system may be represented by imponderables rather than by specific prohibitions. Section 2 is vague and its application arbitrary, and the press are unanimous in their pleas for simplicity and certainty. In their view information should be either secret or not secret, and if it is not secret it should be freely available. What is secret should be defined by statute, as in Sweden and the United States, where individual judgement and dis-cretion are reduced to a minimum, and where exercised are subject to judicial review. Section 2 allows the maximum use of individual dis-cretion on an unlimited number of subjects. For example, section 2(1)(*aa*) refers to the use of official information in a manner 'prejudicial to the safety *or interests* of the State'—a phrase particularly objectionable to the Press Council, who wanted to alter 'interests of the State' to 'security of the nation'. With either expression there is a point at which an individual somewhere has got to exercise a judgement, but there is no doubt that whereas 'the interests of the State' can be stretched to mean almost anything 'the security of the nation' has a much more restricted and definable meaning.

This is borne out by the precision with which it is in fact defined in the U.S., where matters of 'national security' are classified an in Executive Order according to their gravity, with instructions as to which grade of official has power to classify at each level. The U.S. Government thus distinguishes defence and foreign policy secrets from all others, since the interpretation of the remaining excepted categories lies ultimately with the courts.

★

Granted, however, that the difference between an open and a closed system is one of degree, the British system is no longer one which is acceptable in a democracy. There can be few examples of a Departmental Committee in this country expressing itself in quite these terms: 'We found section 2 a mess' (para 88). They were referring partly to what has come to be called its 'catch-all' nature, whereby criminal sanctions can be applied in matters where the criminal law ought not to be operative, and whereby, to continue the quotation, 'a catch-all provision is saved from absurdity in operation only by the sparing exercise of the Attorney-General's discretion to prosecute'; and partly to the fact that its meaning is obscure. In a search for the right balance between openness and secrecy (and the so-called 'open' systems anywhere represent no more than this) it goes too far in the direction of secrecy:

> 'Any law which impinges on the freedom of information in a democracy should be much more tightly drawn.'

On the other hand its simple abolition would go too far in the other direction, by reducing the protection of necessary secrecy, since section 1, as it stands, deals only with espionage, and requires a *purpose* prejudicial to the safety or interests of the State. But those who leak vital information, or are careless with it, are not necessarily spies or traitors.

Accordingly the Franks Committee reached the conclusion that although section 2 should be repealed it should be replaced by 'narrower and more specific provisions'. The lines of reform that it favoured are outlined in page 59. Before coming to them, however, it will be appropriate to give some further description of the position as it exists today, not only with reference to the Official Secrets Acts but in relation to the ordinary day-to-day work of public servants on the one hand and the public (for whom one may to a large extent legitimately read the press) on the other.

THE RESPONSIBILITIES OF PUBLIC AUTHORITIES

Since there is no general right of public access to official information, we must consider the obligations which rest on those who have such information to give or to withhold it.

Central Government

Ministers of Cabinet rank have a strict obligation—though it is one which rests on convention and not on law—to preserve complete secrecy in Cabinet matters, and indeed in departmental matters which require Cabinet consideration or decision. This apart, they have full freedom in their purely departmental capacities, as have the much larger number of ministers and junior ministers who are not in the Cabinet. Naturally their position compels them to be discreet—often to the point of being secretive—but they are not required to sign the same declaration as civil servants regarding the Official Secrets Acts, and since they are the authorizing authority within their own departments they can disclose, or authorize their civil servants to disclose, what they wish.

Civil servants must sign a declaration that they have taken note of the provisions of the Official Secrets Acts, but on the other hand the general code of behaviour by which they are bound now *encourages* openness towards the public and the press, though the permitted limits of disclosure are naturally more restricted in some departments than in others.

This code, embodied in the document known as ESTACODE, is somewhat outside the scope of this essay, as it deals with such matters as a civil servant's permitted 'extra-mural' activities—publications, broadcasts, speeches and the like—in which the unauthorized disclosure of official information, or participation in political controversy, is for obvious reasons forbidden. What is of more significance is that the part of the code dealing with 'Official Information' opens with the following statement:

'General Considerations: The need for greater openness in the work of Government is now widely accepted. Openness in this context means two things:

(a) The fullest possible exposition to Parliament and to the public of the reasons for Government policies and decisions when those policies and decisions are formulated and announced

(b) Creating a better public understanding about the way in which the processes of Government work and about the factual or technical background to Government policies and decisions.'

This general exhortation is, needless to say, qualified in later passages—to the effect that what is made public should rest with 'the appropriate authorities in departments'. This would seem to bring us back to where we started and to justify the critics who say that authorization by privileged and anonymous persons is precisely what they complain of. On the other hand, the statement of principles with which the code begins represents a shift to a far more open attitude than had previously been traditional in the Service.

Moreover it is now possible, because of the voluminous evidence given to the Franks Committee, to examine what information the various departments think ought not to be disclosed; and this does not appear to differ significantly from the categories of information which remain secret in the more professedly open systems.

The question was examined in 1964 by a Working Party whose conclusions[1] may be thought the more significant by virtue of their independence of Government and by the fact that they were representative of the two interests—the law and the press—to whom official secrecy is most repugnant. This was a Joint Working Party of JUSTICE, the British section of the International Commission of Jurists, and the British Committee of the International Press Institute; it was chaired by Sir Hartley Shawcross and comprised three lawyers of considerable experience in public affairs and three editors or experienced newspapermen. Their analysis is perhaps worth quoting at this point:

'It appears that there are five main types of information that we have to consider:

(1) Information prejudicial to the security of the State, e.g. defence and police

(2) Information prejudicial to the national interest, e.g. foreign relations, banking and currency, commodity reserves

(3) Information which through premature disclosure can provide opportunities for unfair financial gain by private interests

(4) Information which is confided to Government departments on promise of non-disclosure

(5) Information which is not prejudicial to the national interest or to

---

[1] Reported in *The Law and the Press*, London: Stevens, 1965, since reprinted.

legitimate private interests, and relates solely to the efficiency or integrity of a Government department or public authority.'

It is not surprising that the JUSTICE Report should have thought it reasonable for the criminal sanctions of the Official Secrets Act to apply to the first two categories; it is universally accepted that these subjects should be on the secret list. Nor could the Report have done other than declare that it was against the interests of good government for the disclosure of information in the fifth category to continue to be treated as a criminal offence. It is more interesting that it should have thought it reasonable for categories (3) and (4) to remain within the provisions of the Act, and thus within the scope of the criminal law. This is said not because the matters comprehended by these categories are unimportant, or that a great deal of information within them ought not to remain confidential; but because *local* authorities are presented with similar problems, which they manage to solve without the aid of criminal sanctions, since the Official Secrets Acts do not apply to local government (See p. 41).

The third category—the use of official information for private gain—is of course almost limitless in its potential application at a time when governments are increasingly concerned with planning, development and investment. It is virtually impossible for many public servants not to acquire information that they could turn to private gain, and this extends to many bodies on the fringe of government, to government contractors and to private consultants. The law on corruption does not deal with these matters unless there is an element of bribery,[2] and it may be agreed that the sanction of internal disciplinary measures only applies to a limited number of those to whom information is available. Moreover the State has a paramount obligation—far exceeding that of any private interest—to ensure complete fairness and impartiality in its dealings with the citizen, and this may be held to warrant the power to invoke criminal sanctions, even in matters in which the security of the state is not in issue.

Much the same may be said of the fourth category—information confided to governments in confidence. It applies equally to great industries, small firms and countless individuals. The Ministry of Agriculture and the Department of Trade and Industry are dependent on a mass of technical, financial and statistical information supplied to them in confidence by industry and commerce; the Department of Education holds over a million personal files of teachers; the Department

---

[2] See p. 60 *infra*. Both the Franks Committee in 1972 and the Royal Commission on Standards in Public Life in 1976 recommended that the law should be strengthened in this regard.

of Health and Social Security has information about the intimate personal circumstances of many millions; and the income tax authorities are familiar with the finances of every taxpayer in the country. The point is too obvious to need labouring. The modern state, especially in its 'welfare' aspects, and in the age of the computer, may abolish personal privacy, and may also abolish personal freedom, unless the sanctions against improper disclosure of personal information are severe.[3]

Considerations of this kind led the JUSTICE Working Party to accept the retention of criminal sanctions in matters that did not 'threaten the security of the state' but would merely be 'prejudicial to the national interest' or involve a breach of trust with individuals.

The fifth category—by which criminal sanctions can in theory be extended to the communication or receipt of official information of any kind—was of course deplored by the Working Party. The point is not pursued here since their view has now received fairly general acceptance, and the Franks proposals suggest the abolition of protection to this category.

Meanwhile, and it may be a long time before the Official Secrets Act is amended, the accessibility of official information to the public will continue to be discretionary; and there are certain areas about which informed public opinion is dissatisfied. One of the most important concerns the administration of prisons. It is common ground that information that would endanger prison security, or facilitate crime or escape, must be secret; but the Official Secrets Act binds all who enter prisons, including chaplains, recognized prison visitors or probation officers, who are restrained from making any comment, public or private, on day-to-day prison administration or the rules and conditions under which prisoners live.

On the whole, however, those who gave evidence to the Franks Committee of a critical or complaining kind were not complaining that the Official Secrets Act stifled the ordinary flow of official information to the public, the question with which we are primarily concerned—or at any rate they did not give examples of the kinds of information which in their view the public were being denied. They were concerned with wider matters which strictly speaking lie outside the province of this essay, but which may be mentioned in passing since 'open government' is a large and indivisible subject.

One group of subjects was really about civil liberties, and arose from

[3] Space does not permit the proper development of the subject of privacy, which was the subject of a separate major investigation which proceeded concurrently with the investigation of the Franks Committee. *Report of the Committee on Privacy*, Chairman: Kenneth Younger, 1972, Cmnd. 5012.

cases which had occurred in the course of political demonstration or on the outer fringes of espionage; another with the reversal of the normal doctrine of British justice, whereby under section 1(2) of the Act of 1911 the burden of proof of innocence rests with the accused; another with the undefined and unsatisfactory position of the media, a matter which we discuss more fully on pages 50 and 52; finally, there was some criticism of a more general kind of secrecy in the administrative *process*, largely from those who favoured legislation of the Swedish or American kind.

For the sake of completeness it should be added that the obligations resting on civil servants are extended to various kinds of persons and bodies to whom the Government must give official information in confidence. They comprise on the one hand a variety of expert individuals outside government, such as members of advisory committees, consultants and researchers; on the other, contractors and sub-contractors engaged in government work. Some are in possession of classified defence information, others of information of no security significance; but as matters stand no distinction is made between them.

Nationalized Industries

These are in a somewhat different position. They exist to carry out commercial operations of a kind inappropriate to direct administration by government departments, and except in matters of broad policy affecting the public interest they have the independence associated with the private sector. Their day-to-day administration, in which one may include the giving or withholding of information, largely follows the practice of private firms and is based on internal rules and discipline.

The *giving* of information to the public is an ordinary matter of commercial public relations, the only difference being that statutory consumer councils give the public certain rights that they do not enjoy in the private sector. These councils are not on the whole regarded with favour by the advocates of open administration and they have recently been the subject of critical discussion.[4] But if they fall short of giving the consumer of their products access to official information they do at least give him a statutory right to demand facts and to make representations.

In the *withholding* of information the position is a little more complicated. There seems to be some doubt about the constitutional

[4] See especially *The Consumer and the Nationalized Industries*, National Consumer Council, HMSO, August 1976 and *The Citizen and the Public Agencies*, JUSTICE, September 1976.

status of *members* of the boards (i.e. the governing bodies) *vis-à-vis* their employees. For example, in evidence to Franks, British Railways said that 'although Members of the Board are persons who hold office under Her Majesty . . . employees of the Board do not hold office under the Crown, and are servants of the Board'. On the other hand the Gas Council said they were advised 'that neither the Chairman nor any Member of the Gas Council holds office under Her Majesty'. The British Steel Corporation took the common sense line of saying 'We have not drawn any specific distinction between the Corporation and its members and employees; what we say applies to all three categories'.

The BSC view is appropriate here, since board members, senior officials and a not inconsiderable number of more junior employees alike are entrusted by government departments with official information —classified and unclassified—in confidence. Since this is so, and since a minister is ultimately responsible for each industry to Parliament, it is thought appropriate that those who handle such information should be required, as civil servants are required, to sign a declaration, which is in fact a variant of the declaration signed by civil servants.[5]

Since, however, such a declaration is not a statutory requirement for all employees of the nationalized industries, but is confined to those selected by the boards themselves as being likely to have access to government information, it could be argued that the Official Secrets Acts only apply to employees of the nationalized industries as they apply to anyone else. There have moreover been differences of opinion as to whether such employees should be required to acknowledge the application of the Acts to Government information only, and if so whether to classified and unclassified information alike, or to inform- ation acquired in the course of their employment—i.e. information generated by the employer and not by the Government—as some declaration forms originally suggested by government departments proposed, and which would have seemed to make the form of declaration wider than the Act itself.[6]

There are, however, two public corporations where legislation specifically applies section 2 of the 1911 Act to everyone concerned—the Post Office and the United Kingdom Atomic Energy Authority. To quote the Post Office Act 1969:

'For the purposes of section 2 of the Official Secrets Act 1911 membership of, or any office of employment under, the authority

---

[5] There are several such variants, applicable, e.g. to visitors to government departments, contractors, advisers and researchers.

[6] These matters were discussed in the Electricity Council's written evidence to Franks, Vol. 2, pp. 190–194 and in Vol. 3 (oral evidence) pp. 45, 46.

shall be deemed to be an office under Her Majesty.'

Legislation establishing the Atomic Energy Authority applies similar provisions to other 'specified bodies corporate'—principally those to whom the Secretary of State has granted permits under the Nuclear Installations Act 1965 and later legislation for certain treatments of irradiated matter and uranium.

These specific provisions would seem to confirm the view that the Official Secrets Acts only apply to the other nationalized industries as they do to the public at large.

Local Government

Here, by contrast, the public have a number of statutory rights, dealing with the audit of accounts, planning applications, access to certain documents and attendance at meetings. They are, in summary:

(1) *Audit*

The Local Government Act 1933 provides that, not less than seven clear days before the annual audit, the accounts and supporting documents must be open to inspection to ratepayers and electors. Anyone entitled to inspect them may, if he wishes, do so through an accountant, and when the audit takes place may lodge an objection.

(2) *Planning applications*

The Town and Country Planning Acts provide that these must be recorded in a register which is open to public inspection, and any member of the public affected by a particular application may see the relevant file and plan, and is entitled to object to the application being granted.

(3) *Access to documents*

The Local Government Act 1972 (Section 228) gives any local elector the right to inspect and make copies of minutes, orders for payments and statements of account.

(4) *Attendance at meetings*

The Public Bodies (Admission to Meetings) Act 1960 provides that the public may attend meetings of local authority councils, and also the comparable meetings of statutory water and health authorities. The Local Government Act 1972 extends this right to attendance at committee meetings.

These statutory requirements are backed up by administrative advice and exhortation.

In 1974 a committee was appointed by the Prime Minister to examine the general question of conduct in local government (Cmnd. 5636). It proposed a draft National Code of Conduct for Councillors, which stressed at the outset the importance of maximum openness as an essential safeguard for honesty and public confidence in local government. But for many years before this the Department had urged local authorities to exercise their maximum rather than their minimum powers in giving information to the public. For example, the publicity given to planning applications can, with imagination, far exceed the statutory requirements; similarly, in planning matters of a different kind—i.e. the future development plans of the authority itself for a town or neighbourhood—publicity can be the minimum required by statute or it can involve public participation of an elaborate kind, with public meetings, exhibitions and invitations for suggestions. Again, the requirement to admit the public to committee meetings can be extended to sub-committees, and a circular issued early in 1975 by the Department urged that this should be done. The same circular exhorted local authorities to improve their lines of communication with the press, and to keep them supplied well in advance with the agenda of meetings and supporting documents.

The speed of advance indicated by the last sentence may be judged from the fact that when the former Ministry of Housing and Local Government last published their own Model Standing Orders for the guidance of local authorities in 1963 they recommended the following:

'All agenda, reports and other documents, and all proceedings of committees and sub-committees, shall be treated as confidential unless and until they become public in the ordinary course of the council's business.'

In a number of ways, therefore, the public have been offered considerable opportunities of access to information. It must be said frankly that they have not, on the whole, availed themselves of these opportunities to a very impressive extent. Their attendance at council and committee meetings is meagre, and invitations to participate in development plans or civic affairs generally draw no great response from individual citizens. On the other hand, organized pressure groups are frequently keen and active, and municipal affairs are normally given a good deal of space in local newspapers.

There are, however, in local as in central government, certain matters which in the interest of fair dealing ought to be kept secret. These are not of an order that could cause grave harm to the community at large if prematurely disclosed[7] but they have in common with some government secrets that their disclosure could result in unfair financial gain by individuals, or in a breach of confidence with individual citizens.

The first of these may be seen in the exercise of certain planning powers, in which the disclosure of policy could result in foreknowledge that the price of land may rise; or it could result un undeserved loss, since if it is known that land may be developed for some new purpose, those who own property on it may find it unsaleable at current market price. The second arises because intimate personal details are confided to local authorities, as they are to government departments; education, housing and social services departments all have information about family finances, physical or mental health or, at the bottom of the social scale, social inadequacy and poverty.

The possession of so much information of this latter kind raises an interesting question on which Standing Orders are not always specific, concerning the right, not of the public, but of an elected councillor to see 'official information' in the form of internal files. The Model Standing Order of the Department suggests that a councillor should be allowed to inspect documents *for the purpose of his duty but not otherwise*, and this follows case law, which has established in principle the right of a local authority to withhold official information from a councillor, it being a matter of interpretation whether the information is necessary to enable him to perform his duties properly.[8] Nevertheless, the point is raised from time to time as a matter of dispute. In 1974 a county councillor was denied access to a file in the Social Services Department on the ground that it contained confidential reports from medical officers, though subsequently he was permitted to see it. But should the Hippocratic oath have any less validity when the doctor concerned is a public employee whose opinion must go on a local authority file?[9] And should election to representative office entitle a man to see confidential personal information about those who elected him?

In spite of handling so much sensitive information, local authorities have managed to preserve a creditable record for discretion and trust-worthiness without the criminal sanctions which apply in the civil service, though it is noteworthy that the Franks Report (para. 206) did not rule out the possibility of ultimately extending the criminal law to the local government field.

[7] There are exceptions, since local authorities, like nationalized industries, may from time to time be trusted with government information in confidence. See Franks Report para. 206.

[8] See *R. v. Barnes Borough Council ex parte Conlon* (1938) 3 All E.R. 226, in which three previous cases are cited.

[9] For a recent decision about the application of professional privilege in relation to the advice given by such advisers to those employing them see *Alfred Crompton v. Customs and Excise Commissioners* (1974), A.C. 405.

THE SANCTION OF INVESTIGATION

This essay deals primarily with the release of official information to the public as a deliberate act, but the account would be incomplete if no reference were made to information that is made available as a result of investigation, which may take place either as a matter of common practice, as with certain parliamentary select committees, or under pressure of complaint, as with the Parliamentary and Local Government Commissioners.

Even taking into account the trend towards openness which we have discussed, the Government of a country in which there is no right of public access may be thought to be in a privileged position, since it is they who decide whether and if so to what extent to release information, and they do not have to show the *need* for secrecy. Governmental authorities in the U.K., however—the Cabinet apart—are by no means immune from scrutiny, but may be called upon to give an account of their stewardship in a way which can require them to disclose information involuntarily.

The Cabinet

The Cabinet is in a category apart, not only because it is the apex of the governmental system, carrying ultimate responsibility for the decisions of the Government of the day, but because it works within the doctrine of collective responsibility, which demands the strictest privacy for its deliberations. Accordingly, as soon as working papers become Cabinet documents they become secret, and even the Franks Committee, which in general would have preferred to minimize secrecy, and to shift the emphasis from criminal sanctions to internal discipline, did not suggest that the full rigour of the Official Secrets Acts should not apply to Cabinet papers.[1]

At the time of writing there is a police investigation—an internal investigation having proved inconclusive—into the disclosure of a Cabinet paper on the payment of social security benefits to the editor of

[1] A recent statement of intent by the Government (November 1976) has in fact modified the Franks view. See p. 64.

New Society, who subsequently published it. If the person responsible were identified he would of course be liable to prosecution. The disclosure of Cabinet *proceedings* by Cabinet Ministers is a different matter, being governed primarily by convention and not by law. The complexity of the legal position was shown by the judgement of the Lord Chief Justice in the case of the Crossman Diaries, which is discussed on page 54.

Government Departments

But the ordinary processes of executive government, which involve ministers and civil servants alike, may on occasion be liable to investigation—indeed 'inquisition' would not be an inappropriate word.

Two permanent select committees of the House of Commons have the power to investigate departmental administration, to examine witnesses and to call for documents—the Public Accounts Committee and the Expenditure Committee, which include members of all the main political parties. Both, as their names imply, are intended to be instruments of financial control, but both, as is inevitable, go far beyond their original function of scrutinizing past expenditure or examining future estimates.

The Public Accounts Committee, whose history goes back over a hundred years, meets regularly throughout the year to examine how the money granted by Parliament has been spent, and it works in collaboration with the staff of the Comptroller and Auditor-General, an official who enjoys the independent standing of a judge. The Expenditure Committee, successor to the former 'Estimates Committee', works through six sub-committees, each dealing with a group of subjects, and has a free hand to select departmental estimates with a view to seeing, *inter alia*, how the policy which shaped the estimates can be most effectively and economically implemented. Both committees, in the course of the investigations, become closely involved not only with administration but with policy—the dichotomy between the two being largely mythical—and both are entitled to examine ministers and officials alike.

The result is that official information, and information on which policy is based, is made available to the representatives of Parliament, and subsequently to the press and public through the publication annually of a full account, including minutes of evidence, of the committees' investigations.

On the other hand, proceedings are not always distinguished for their ease or urbanity and, as is well known, the reports of the Standing Select Committees have on occasion been remarkably uninhibited in their criticism of departments. This is doubtless as it should be and in any case is not our immediate concern. More to the point is the fact that secrecy may prevail, or may be alleged to prevail, over the information with which the Select Committees are provided.

A case in point occurred in September 1976, when the education sub-committee of the Expenditure Committee found not only that the Department of Education and Science was unduly secretive in its long-term planning—in the sense that it did not sufficiently involve outside interest groups and the general public—but that it was also secretive about what it let the Select Committee itself know. The chairman complained, for example, they were refused access to some major planning papers, including one relating to the Programme Analysis and Review. A brief paragraph cannot properly deal with a complex dispute,[2] but it may be justifiable to say first, that the decision regarding the PAR was ministerial rather than official; and second—a remark of general application—that the circumstances of a public inquisition may not encourage senior civil servants to speak altogether freely. People generally are not necessarily at their most informative when they have to choose every word with care, knowing that what they say will appear in print—a simple enough point, but one which is fundamental to the whole matter of open government, and constitutes one of its limitations.

There are other Select Committees of more recent creation, some of which, like that on Science and Technology, deal with a subject affecting many departments, and are principally concerned with 'informing the House' on current developments; others are concerned with a particular department, e.g. Overseas Development or Agriculture, their brief being to 'consider the activities' of the department concerned and to report to the House with minutes of evidence, thus giving them virtually unlimited power of scrutiny.

Select Committees consider broad issues of policy, while the Parliamentary Commissioner for Administration investigates alleged maladministration in matters without policy significance. In doing so he is given access to official information which may thereafter become public in his reports. There is a proviso that a minister may give notice in writing that disclosure would be prejudicial to the interest of the state or otherwise contrary to the public interest, but in the normal run of cases his published reports give 'full but anonymized texts of reports on individual cases'. The British ombudsman works under a number of

[2] It is more adequately dealt with in the *Times Educational Supplement*, 24 September 1976.

limitations compared with his counterpart in some other countries. He is empowered to investigate complaints of alleged maladministration in government departments, but may only receive complaints through the channel of a Member of Parliament; and he is excluded from investigating the armed forces, the police and prisons, the nationalized industries, local government and the national health service (though under later legislation the last two have acquired 'ombusmen' of their own). Nevertheless, in the year 1975 he received 928 complaints from Members and dealt with a further 219 carried forward from 1974, a total of 1,147. More than half these cases, in spite of the 'filter' of the Member of Parliament, turned out to be outside his jurisdiction, but 321 cases were investigated and the result reported upon.

Nationalized Industries

The administration of the nationalized industries is scrutinized by a third Select Committee, whose original terms of reference have also become strikingly enlarged.

The Select Committee on Nationalized Industries, which has the power to summon ministers, civil servants and the heads of the industries themselves, has been active and thorough. During the first twenty years of its existence (1956–76) it has presented some twenty-five major Reports to the House of Commons. Most of these have dealt with individual industries, the Airways Corporations having been the subject of three reports, the National Coal Board and the Post Office two each, whilst nearly all the others have been before the Committee once, as have the Bank of England and the Independent Broadcasting Authority. The Committee have also dealt with 'across-the-board' subjects, namely Ministerial Control of the Nationalized Industries (1968), Relations with the Public (1971) and Procedures governing Capital Investment (1973). Their voluminous reports and minutes of evidence, which leave little unsaid about internal administration, policy and commercial results, are freely available.

This enlargement of their original functions, which has been gradual and almost unnoticed, is not without interest in the general context of open government. The first Select Committee was appointed to 'examine the Report and Accounts . . .' and its object was simply to 'inform Parliament', but as early as November 1956 the government spokesman, pressed for examples of what the Committee might look at, instanced the devolution of authority within the industry, the techniques of managerial efficiency, the recruitment and training of staff, relations

45

with the public and with other industries and the Boards' non-remunerative responsibilities. The 'Observations' which were the customary conclusions of the earlier reports gradually turned into 'Recommendations', and there was a notable development in 1966 when the Committee was increased in size and was authorized to appoint sub-committees with important delegated powers. As another government spokesman had said during the 1956 debate 'their scope is impossible to define with precision . . .', they were 'essentially pragmatic' and 'in the democratic process we have to feel our way'.

It is difficult to assess the value of the Committee's output, which has been enormous and costly, but whose reception has varied from enthusiasm to disappointment. Their reports are avidly received by the press, who regard their publication as one of the relatively few occasions when the veil of secrecy is drawn aside, and in the context of our subject this may be one of their main justifications. Some individual Chairmen of the Boards of the nationalized industries have also welcomed them with enthusiasm, as providing insights into their affairs which had escaped their own notice; Lord Robens, when Chairman of the National Coal Board, was especially complimentary in this sense, admitting that he had changed his mind about the Committee's value. On the other hand, many of the official published replies of the industries have been somewhat petulant, rebutting criticism and complaining that the Committee frequently under-estimated what was being done, and it does not seem that very much has been changed as a result of what the Committee has had to say. What is quite certain is that Parliament as such has shown little interest in the reports, however much the minds of individual members may have been 'informed' by them. They are not automatically debated, and in fact debates on any of them have been few and cursory. The matter is perhaps worth closer investigation.

There is as yet no ombudsman for the nationalized industries and the task of remedying grievances falls to the network of separate consumer consultative councils referred to on page 37. Opinion differs as to their effectiveness but it has not on the whole been favourable.[3] They are criticized, among other things, for being too remote, too little known and too much 'in the pockets' of the managements of the industries themselves, as well as for being insufficiently representative. Whether such criticisms are justified or not is to some extent irrelevant, since the councils can only hope to be effective on a basis of public confidence. The problem has long been a troublesome one and it is timely that JUSTICE should have made a report with recommendations based on a

---

[3] See footnote to p. 37.

two-year study.[4]

The Report concludes that the consultative councils have by no means failed but it agrees, first, that they need strengthening if they are to conform to the authors' own criteria of 'visibility, accessibility, independence, expertise, authority and representativeness'; and second, that in this particular respect the threads of all the industries and public corporations need to be drawn together and to be held in one pair of hands—those of a high official comparable to the ombudsman. On balance, and while acknowledging their several virtues, the authors of the Report reject various alternative solutions, such as a concentration of the work into the hands of all-purpose regional consultative councils, or their replacement by regional ombudsmen, by local authorities or by the Office of Fair Trading. None of these, they think, would serve the public better than the existing councils provided the latter could be standardized, publicized and better staffed, and certain gaps repaired and anomalies abolished; and provided also that this structure for the remedying of grievances could be completed by a Nationalized Industries and Agencies Commissioner whose position would be closely analagous to that of the Parliamentary Commissioner.

The JUSTICE recommendations are controversial and at the time of writing have had a somewhat mixed reception, but it is common ground that they have done a useful service it publicizing and clarifying an important matter.

Local Government and the National Health Service

In 1974 the ombudsman principle was extended to local government and to the national health service.

In the former, 'Local Commissioners' accept complaints from elected councillors, just as the PCA accepts them from MPs, though in this case the complainant may have the right of direct access to the Commissioner if it can be shown that a local councillor refuses 'unreasonably' to pass on the complaint. Local Commissioners are barred from investigating complaints about the police or, in general, about policy decisions of local authorities or technical decisions within professional competence; they can, however, examine whether the council or professional officer concerned considered all the relevant evidence, i.e. whether the policy or technical decision was competently based. The Local Commissioners' main purpose is to protect individuals from maladministration arising from delay, neglect, incompetence or prejudice, though they may not

[4] *The Citizen and the Public Agencies* (*Remedying Grievances*), 1976. (Chairman of Committee: Professor J. F. Garner).

consider the *merits* of a decision if it has been reached fairly. Reports are available to press and public.

As to national health, the minister is wholly responsible for the service in that he provides the money and may give directives of a general—i.e. non-professional—nature, but management is in the hands of regional boards and hospital management committees which, though nominally appointed by the minister, are representative in character— notably of the various branches of the medical, dental and allied professions—and which have an independent legal status (National Health Service Act 1946 Part II). The National Health Service (Reorganization) Act 1973 provides for 'Health Service Commissioners' who are ombudsmen in all but name, and some of whose powers and duties are in fact transposed from the Parliamentary Commissioner Act 1967. But the functions of the Health Service Commissioners are, at any rate to start with, being exercised by the Local Commissioners who were first on the ground.[5]

---

[5] An up-to-date account of the early work of the Local Commissioners will appear in a forthcoming booklet to be published by the Royal Institute of Public Administration.

RESPONSIBILITIES OF THE PRESS AND PUBLIC

Throughout this essay there are considerable areas where 'the public' could more properly read 'the press', since few ordinary citizens have the knowledge, ability or time—or even the inclination—to go in pursuit of official information, whereas it is an important function of the press to do so on their behalf. For the next few pages, therefore, we speak simply of the press. The information we are considering is of two kinds —that which is voluntarily given to the press by the Government, and that which the press discovers for itself, possibly by devious means and to the embarrassment of authority.

The Westminster Lobby Correspondents

One of the main recognized channels of communication is the 'Press Lobby' of the House of Commons, to which rather more than a hundred journalists are accredited, the majority from daily newspapers, others from the Sunday papers, the press agencies and the broadcasting networks. The Lobby is a curious institution, difficult to describe in straightforward terms, as it is governed by convention, mutual trust and unspoken assumptions rather than by rules, though its members have devised a code of rules for themselves, designed principally to preserve the relationship of trust between themselves and the politicians and civil servants whom they meet, and on which the effective working of the Lobby mainly depends.

Twice-daily briefings are given by the Prime Minister's press staff, and there are other regular briefings by departmental ministers, by the Leader of the House of Commons and the Leader of the Opposition. Ministers accompanied by their civil servants also hold special meetings with the Lobby to discuss policy on forthcoming legislation. Lobby correspondents are also supplied with a great deal of documentary material, often before it is available to the House of Commons itself. The Lobby, however, is not simply a passive recipient of whatever information those in authority choose to give it. Some meetings are arranged by invitation of the Lobby, or a Minister might seek such an invitation, for ministers need the Lobby as much as the Lobby needs ministers.

Formalized briefings, however, are probably less important than the network of personal contacts, often of personal friendships, which develop between journalists and politicians. A feature of both the formal briefings and of the personal contacts is that a very high proportion of what is told to journalists is understood to be 'non-attributable'—it may be freely used but the source must not be named.

These arrangements, unconventional and haphazard as they may seem, work to the satisfaction of both sides. They are, however, open to some fairly obvious criticism. A relatively small and elite corps of journalists are naturally content with an arrangement whereby they enjoy the confidence and friendship of important people. But such an arrangement is only possible on the basis of strict confidence, and the press are very much in the hands of their hosts. It is indeed a host-guest relationship, with all that that implies. Having said this, it is not easy, within the existing legislative framework, to suggest how the arrangements could be improved.[1]

Outside the Westminster Lobby there are other important specialist groups of journalists who get privileged treatment, e.g. the industrial, educational or financial correspondents. Moreover, a vast amount of information in the form of press notices, press conferences and briefings is given out by departments to general reporters and news desks, and departments maintain well-staffed public relations departments and information offices. The press do not, however, have direct access to departmental officials, let alone to official documents.

Voluntary Agreement of the Press to Keep Secrets

This aspect of the relationship between Government and press concerns editors rather than reporters—there being certain matters which, from time to time, they are asked not to publish in the interest of national security. This is done through a form of voluntary censorship, exercised by a body representative of the press and broadcasting interests on the one hand and the Government and the armed forces on the other, and known as the Services, Press and Broadcasting Committee.

Its function is to warn the media that it would be against the interests of national security to publish certain information and to seek the media's own consent to non-disclosure. Such requests, which take the form of what are called 'D-notices', have no statutory force and are not provided

---

[1] For a full account of the Lobby see Jeremy Tunstall, *The Westminster Lobby Correspondent*, London: Routledge & Kegan Paul, 1970.

for in the Official Secrets Acts, though to ignore them could of course bring an offending editor within the purview of the Acts. The arrangement goes back some sixty years in one form or another, and until comparatively recent times was not regarded by the press as a threat to their freedom or as a kind of non-statutory extension of the Official Secrets Acts. It was, on the contrary, a singularly harmonious arrangement, which gave satisfaction to both sides. During the 1960s, however, tensions came into the relationship, the press thinking that the Government were tending to depart from the strict use of D-notices to preserve essential secrets, and were permitting their use to suppress information inconvenient or embarrassing to themselves.

At first, the press's justification was that a number of D-notices had been issued on subjects which were currently being freely reported in foreign newspapers, though as late as 1965 the Committee of JUSTICE did not consider these to be serious, and were able to speak of the D-notice system in commendatory terms. In 1967, however, two more serious episodes shattered the relationship of mutual trust, and it has been slow to mend. One sought to place an embargo on the publication of information about the Foreign Office traitors, Philby, Burgess and Maclean, although the fullest information was obviously available to the country to which they had defected; in this case two newspapers took their courage in both hands and published, and were not prosecuted. The other case, which caused a much greater furore, and which brought a much-resented intervention by the Prime Minister, centred on a report by the *Daily Express* about the 'vetting' of overseas cables by the Ministry of Defence. So serious did this become that a small committee of Privy Councillors was appointed to examine the facts.[2] These proved to be extremely tangled and to be shot through with misunderstandings and half-truths. It would be out of place to attempt to summarize them here. But the fact that the affair could happen at all illustrates the delicacy of voluntary arrangements based on trust and good sense, and the need for greater sensitivity on the part of authority in a free democracy.

The D-Notice system continues, but the media are more suspicious of it than they used to be, believing that the incidents of the 1960s marked a turning away from security secrets, in whose suppression they willingly co-operated, to the suppression of information which did not prejudice national security, but which the Government would prefer to hide.

[2] Report of a Committee of Privy Councillors appointed to inquire into 'D' Notice matters. Cmnd. 3309, 1967.

51

Statutory Obligation on the Press to Keep Secrets

Naturally the press is not content to gather its news solely in the Westminster Lobby or from Government public relations officers. Reporters will inevitably go behind the scenes and sniff out, if they can, the exciting, the controversial and if possible the scandalous, and will on occasion take risks in order to publish something they think is in the public interest, or simply to file a good story; and, as we have seen, one of their complaints is that the risks are difficult to calculate owing to the uncertain, and potentially capricious, operation of section 2. The Attorney General's power to authorize prosecution may be very rarely used but it can never be completely ignored.

One particular risk however, was removed by legislation in 1939. Before that date a journalist would have had to reveal his sources of information, or suffer the penalties for not doing so, if charged with an offence under either section 1 or section 2 of the 1911 Act. An Official Secrets Act of 1939 restricted this power of interrogation to section 1, i.e. to cases of alleged espionage and not to offences concerning the more general 'interests of the state'.

The most important case in recent years occurred in 1971, commonly referred to as the *Sunday Telegraph* case. A journalist, Jonathan Aitken, came into possession of a document which was a military appreciation by the Defence Adviser to the British High Commission in Lagos of the prospect of a successful termination of the civil war by the Federal forces, and the *Sunday Telegraph* accepted it for publication. Three men were prosecuted under section 2, Colonel Cairns, who originally sent the document to the U.K. (though not to Mr. Aitken personally), the editor of the newspaper and Mr. Aitken himself, and were tried at the Central Criminal Court. The trial itself is described in detail in Mr. Aitken's book *Officially Secret*,[3] and its story is impossible to summarize briefly without distortion. It was a somewhat tangled tale of mixed motives, indiscretions, misunderstandings and wrestlings with conscience. The essential facts in the present context are that the communicating and receiving of the document did not affect national security, though they did affect friendly relations between the British and Nigerian Governments, and seriously embarrassed British ministers and civil servants, who had behaved with complete propriety. Secondly, the jury found Cairns not guilty of making an unauthorized communication, and Aitken and the newspaper not guilty of receiving and communicating the document 'knowing or having reasonable grounds to believe' that they were acting in contravention of the Act. Thirdly, the judge, whose

[3] London: Weidenfield and Nicolson, 1971.

summing-up had been strongly favourable to the defendants, ended the case with some caustic observations about section 2, saying, in a much quoted remark, that the Act was just approaching its sixtieth year and that it was time it was pensioned off.

It was shortly after this case that the Franks Committee started its work, though the case was not, as is often supposed, the *cause* of the Committee's appointment. This had been decided on before the trial began, but it was thought proper to postpone the beginning of its work until the *Sunday Telegraph* case was over.

There was another notorious case in the following year, associated with the name of the *Railway Gazette*. This was of a different order, since it was clear that a document had been stolen from a government department and given to the editor, and a warrant for arrest was accordingly issued under the Theft Act, and not, as would have been equally possible, under the Official Secrets Act. But in the event the case did not come to trial, since the evidence proved insufficient to proceed to a charge. The document which had come into the hands of the editor, and which was used as the basis for an article in the *Sunday Times*, dealt with a plan to close down 40 per cent of the railway system of the country within the succeeding 10 years. It was in fact one of a number of alternative contingency plans, and not a proposal for action, but none the less it was dealing with a matter of high public interest. The point in the context of this essay is that the police raided the offices of the *Railway Gazette*, and detectives closely questioned the editor of the *Sunday Times*, warning him that its *receipt* had been in contravention of the Officials Secrets Act. Both editors, however, refused, as they were entitled, to disclose the source of their information, and the case petered out.

Scholars and Researchers

These constitute the other section of the 'public' who most need access to official records. Their lot has been a hard one, as the predilection of the civil service for secrecy has been projected to the records of past deeds. Until recently, to the great irritation of authors and scholars, public documents were closed to inspection for a period of 50 years, and the rule was strictly enforced regardless of the quality of the material in question. It is said in defence of a long period of restriction that the doctrine of collective Cabinet responsibility demands that papers should remain confidential during the life-time of the participants. While this may be a plausible argument for restricting Cabinet papers, it hardly justified the withholding of departmental papers with no bearing either on national security or Cabinet secrecy. Most scholars who have tried to get access to official records can bear witness not only to the triviality of the information they were seeking in terms of national security, but to anomalies such as the information being freely available in libraries overseas, or by word of mouth from participants in the events.

In 1970 the fifty-year rule was relaxed to some extent and became a thirty-year rule, which makes comparatively little difference to those interested in recent or contemporary history. The relaxation was, however, accompanied by a statement of intent by the Head of the civil service that sympathetic consideration would be given to requests within the thirty-year period for the purposes of research which would assist in the training of administrators, and later for the purposes of normal academic research. Exceptions would be the reasonable ones of Cabinet papers, topics still within the field of active political controversy, and those which bore on national security.

Here is another straw in the wind which is blowing in favour of more open government and greater public access to information, even though the concessions seem unduly cautious and the scholar still has more hurdles to surmount than seems reasonable. Thirty years is still a long time.

Ministerial Memoirs

Meanwhile, dissatisfaction on the part of objective scholars is increased by the fact that Members of Parliament, and notably Cabinet ministers in their voluminous memoirs, seem able to breach the rules which apply to civil servants and scholars without much difficulty. Drafts are supposed to be cleared by the Secretary to the Cabinet before publication, and amendments have in practice been made which have removed the actual quotation of Cabinet papers, though not revelations of personal differences in Cabinet. Nevertheless, a good deal has been published under eminent authorship of a kind that could result in criminal prosecution for the ordinary person.

But although a number of Cabinet ministers have sat somewhat loosely to the convention of Cabinet secrecy the late Richard Crossman deliberately and openly flouted it, for what appeared to himself to be good reasons. The Secretary to the Cabinet withheld his endorsement of the publication of the Diaries, and the Attorney-General, on behalf of the Government, sought an injunction to prevent the publication of further instalments in the *Sunday Times* and ultimate publication in book form by Jonathan Cape. An injunction was granted by the Divisional Court in June 1975, but the defendants went to the Appeal Court, which heard the case on 27-28 June but reserved judgement until the new Law Term. It was eventually delivered by the Lord Chief Justice on 1 October 1975.

The Court of Appeal noted that the convention that had in the past governed the publication of Cabinet proceedings by ex-ministers,

'flowed from the two complementary principles of the collective responsibility of the Government as a whole and the personal responsibility of individual ministers'

and that it derived not from the Official Secrets Acts, which were not in issue, but from the 'inherent needs of Government'. It was perfectly 'honourable and legitimate' for Cabinet ministers to publish their memoirs provided they were cleared by the Secretary to the Cabinet, but there had been no previous attempt to define the *extent* to which Cabinet papers should be treated as secret or confidential. The matter was governed by convention and this, in the last analysis, was based on conscience.

It is interesting—to digress for a moment from narrative—that it was accepted without question that the Official Secrets Acts did not apply to this publication, a point conceded both by the Secretary to the Cabinet and by the Attorney-General.[4] Clearly the Government were not anxious to have the point argued before the Court, yet it would appear to the layman that there was a point to be argued. No doubt Crossman, as a Cabinet minister, was a legitimate 'authorizing authority', but it is not clear whether he ever gave a specific authorization or whether this was considered to persist after he had ceased to be a Cabinet minister and even to be inherited by his literary executors after his death. It might have been of advantage for the Court to have been able to deal with the point specifically.[5]

The Attorney-General's case for an injunction was based on the fact that the Crossman Diaries disclosed not only differences of individual views among Cabinet ministers, but the confidential advice given to them by senior civil servants, and the discussion surrounding the appointment or transfer of these same officials. The Attorney contended that when a minister received information in confidence the Court could restrain publication. The Court upheld this contention in principle, but

[4] See Lord Widgery's judgement in *A. G. v. Jonathan Cape Ltd.* (1975) 3 W.L.R. 606, pp. 610C and 615F and G.

[5] It is of some interest that para. 26 of the Report of the Committee of Privy Counsellors on Ministerial Memoirs (Cmnd. 6386, January 1976) states that 'No prosecution under the Official Secrets Acts has been instituted against a Minister or ex-Minister'.

held that the application of the principle was not absolute but that its application depended on circumstances.

In these particular circumstances the Court had to consider whether 'the public interest' would be adversely affected by publication, particularly in view of the fact that ten years had elapsed since the events under discussion. The Court was of the opinion that it would not, and even that 'today's Cabinet would not be inhibited, even though some are the same people'.

There was, moreover, no ground in law to prevent the publication of civil servants' advice or discussion of their postings. These were matters of 'good sense and good taste'. The Court had 'no power to restrain a breach of confidence except in extreme cases where national security was involved', and this did not apply in the present case.

Accordingly the application for an injunction was refused so far as the contents of Volume 1 of the Diaries were concerned (these being all that had been under consideration) but the publication of subsequent volumes, or instalments, of the Diaries would be considered on their merits and on the circumstances obtaining at the time of publication.

Mr. Crossman appeared to interpret open government as meaning that people should know exactly *how* they were governed and what went on behind the scenes, warts and all; he cheerfully swept aside what he regarded as the cobwebs of convention, in the supposed interests of posterity. It is a legitimate point of view, and the Court upheld that he acted within the existing law, at any rate so far as the Diaries so far prepared for publication were concerned. Clearly when a man has no inhibitions about what he says of colleagues or servants, and when he writes from the centre of events, we learn a great deal that we did not know before, and while much of it may be unedifying or disillusioning much is fascinating. Crossman may have been right in supposing that future historians would find his diaries an indispensible source.

On the other hand, it is a haphazard way of moving towards more open government to rely on the subjective views, and possibly prejudices, of men of widely varying talents and deficiencies. As was said in evidence by the Association of First Division Civil Servants to a Committee of Privy Councillors in December 1975:

'Open government should come to deliberate choice and not as the unintended consequence of a proliferation of personal memoirs'.

This Committee, appointed by the Prime Minister in the wash of the Crossman affair, was known as the Committee of the Privy Council on Ministerial Memoirs, and reported in January 1976. It recommended that ministerial authors should be precluded for fifteen[6]—instead of the usual thirty—years from publishing information in the following categories:

First, information which might prejudice national security *at the time of proposed publication*—a matter which the author himself, being out of office, would be unable to judge; second, information which would be injurious to relations with other countries; and third, information destructive of the confidential relationship upon which the system of government is based, i.e. the relationship between ministers and their colleagues or their advisers, in the civil service or outside it.

These were accepted by the Prime Minister as satisfactory working rules. Had they existed earlier, and had Richard Crossman accepted them, they would have inhibited much of what he wrote. Acceptance remains, however, a matter of honour, since although the law is, as now appears, unable to deal with ministerial indiscretions there is no proposal to amend it.

---

[6] The fifteen years to be extended if public servants involved were still in office.

THE FRANKS REPORT

It is now (early 1977) over four years since the Franks Report was published, and so far none of its recommendations has been implemented. The main political parties have committed themselves in principle to new legislation, and a great deal of preparatory work has been done, or is in progress, in the background. Both parties agree that it is unsatisfactory that the validity of an Act of Parliament should rest upon the fact that it is hardly ever used, however frequently its terms may be breached. It may be a British absurdity that happens to work reasonably well, but on such sensitive matters, and at a time of heightened political criticism, this is hardly sufficient justification, and it is perhaps significant that 1976 saw the establishment of a new pressure group—the All-Party Committee on Freedom of Information—whose purpose is to campaign for a 'Freedom of Information and Privacy Act for the United Kingdom'. Because of the wide support that it attracted it has now been reconstituted as a purely parliamentary committee, the other members having formed a national Campaign for Freedom of Information in its support.

A point of interest in the Committee's proposals is that they explicitly link greater freedom of information with greater personal privacy, two concepts that are not always in harmony. In other words they aim to link Franks with Younger,[1] and since these two Committees, though sitting contemporaneously and studying related matters, left each other's subject severely alone in their Reports, it is interesting to find them joined together in the All-Party Committee's recently published brochure.[2]

Four years ago the Franks Report, arising as it did out of the observations of the Fulton Committee and coinciding with the *cause célèbre* of the *Sunday Telegraph*, raised a good deal of interest. It then faded from from public consciousness, but has once again become the current coin of political discussion because of the popular scandals of the Crossman Diaries and the disclosure of Cabinet papers to the editor of *New Society*, followed by the announcement that the Prime Minister had appointed a committee of senior ministers and civil servants to look at the whole

[1] Report of a Committee on Privacy under the chairmanship of Sir Kenneth Younger, Cmnd. 5012, July 1972.

[2] *Making Trust a Two-Way Street*, April 1976, published from 8 Elsiedene Road, London N21, April 1976.

subject again. At the time of writing the Franks Report is often mentioned in the newspapers and on the air. What, then, does it say?

The Franks Report – Summary

The Committee's purpose, as it emerged after taking massive written and oral evidence, was to put something in place of section 2 that would be 'more limited' and 'more certain in operation'. The possibility of doing this had, in evidence, been strongly disputed by government witnesses, on the ground that it was manifestly impossible to foresee every circumstance that might injure the interests of the nation (leaving aside espionage, which is dealt with by section 1). This, however, is a difficulty which must arise in reverse in the 'open' systems, where exceptions have to be stated to the general right of access. The Committee declined to be deterred by it.

They accepted without question that 'the present law is unsatisfactory and that it should be changed so that criminal sanctions are retained only to protect what is of real importance.'[3]

They did not go as far as some critics of the 1911 Act—especially the press—would have wished, and propose that section 2 should simply be abolished and not replaced. Certainly they recommended that it should be repealed, but they proposed an entirely new statute, which they would call the 'Official Information Act', which would restrict the application of criminal sanctions to six closely defined categories of information. The first three categories relate to the universally familiar matters of:

(1) Defence and internal security
(2) Foreign relations
(3) Currency and the reserves

but with the proviso that the information concerned shall have been officially classified[4] and that in the event of a prosecution the court must be satisfied that it fell within the correct classification.

[3] Report para. 275. Paras. 176 and 277 go on to outline the Committee's recommendations, which are then set out in detail in para. 278, of which what follows is a summary.

[4] The details of classification, de-classification and authority to classify and de-classify, are complicated and technical. They get in the way of straightforward narrative and are peripheral to the subject of open government in the broad sense. They are none the less important, and a note on them, as they exist and as the Franks Report thought they ought to be, is accordingly included as an appendix.

The remaining three are:

(4) Maintenance of law and order, that is information likely to help in the commission of offences; likely to help prison escape or affect security; and likely to prevent or impede the apprehension of offenders

(5) Cabinet documents, i.e. documents submitted for the consideration of Cabinet, and documents recording the proceedings or conclusions of Cabinet, irrespective of subject matter

(6) The confidence of the citizen, i.e. information given to the Government by private individuals or concerns, whether given by reason of compulsory powers or otherwise, and whether or not given on an express or implied basis of confidence.

There follow recommendations about the use of official information for private gain, by a Crown servant, government contractor or other person entrusted with official information in confidence, or by a recipient of such information (using it for private gain) who knew that it had been improperly given. These recommendations, which would in effect be an extension of the law on corruption, were later to be quoted (in 1976) by the Royal Commission on Standards of Conduct in Public Life (Cmnd. 6524) and were used to support the Royal Commission's own proposal that the Prevention of Corruption Acts, as they apply to the public sector, should be amended and consolidated into a new Act which would *inter alia* make it a criminal offence to use official information for private gain irrespective of whether there was any element of bribery.

The Report goes on to define at some length the responsibilities which should rest on various categories of persons, and the defences which should be available to them in the event of prosecution. The categories are, first, Crown servants,[5] second, government contractors and others entrusted with official information in confidence and third, the ordinary citizen. In the case of the last named the mere receipt of information, knowing it to have been given in contravention of the Act, would no longer be an offence, but its communication would continue to be so, though what the prosecution would have to prove, and what the citizen could say in his own defence, is set out at some length.

The last subject with which the Report deals, other than penalties for contravention of the Official Information Act, is control over the institution of prosecutions. It will be recalled that the existing law

[5] Defined as ministers of the Crown, members of the Home Civil Service and the Diplomatic Service, members of the Armed Forces, members of police forces and members of the Atomic Energy Authority and the Post Office.

requires the authorization of the Attorney-General, and there are those to whom this is unacceptable because the Attorney is a politician and a member of the Government. To them the mere convention that he is non-partisan is insufficient, and they would prefer the authority to lie with the Director of Public Prosecutions.

The relationship between these two officers in England and Wales[6] is in fact close though complicated, since statutes confer the power on one or the other without apparent principle, and even where the Director is the authority he will customarily consult the Attorney on cases of difficulty; moreover the Director is formally responsible to the Attorney, who in turn is responsible to Parliament for the Director's actions. But what was of more relevance to the Franks Committee was that in their view some of the six categories of offence which they were proposing were in essence political, in that they related to sensitive matters of public policy, and that *political* experience, and direct accountability to Parliament, was positively desirable in the authorizing officer. They accepted that the existing blanket power of the Attorney over the existing provisions of section 2 was undesirable, but thought that their own proposed narrowing down of section 2 to six specific categories allowed a distinction to be made betw.en 'ordinary' offences, relating to law and order and private gain, where prosecution should be authorized by the Director, and the politically sensitive subjects of defence and national security, foreign relations, currency and the reserves, Cabinet documents and the confidence of the citizen, where authorization should remain with the Attorney.

The Franks Report – Comment

The most obvious criticism of the Franks Committee concerns not their Report but their terms of reference, i.e. it is a criticism of the Conservative Home Secretary of the day. On their own showing their appointment 'can be traced directly to the Report of the Fulton Committee on the Civil Service'. But the Fulton recommendation was that:

'the Government should set up an enquiry to make recommendations for getting rid of unnecessary secrecy in this country. Clearly the Official Secrets Acts would need to be *included in such a review*' (present author's italics).

Unfortunately the part became the whole, and the Franks terms of reference were 'to review the operation of section 2 of the Official

---

[6] The position in Scotland is quite different (Report paras. 246 and 256).

Secrets Act 1911 and to make recommendations'.

There were tempted to exceed their duty, since many witnesses urged them to consider recommending legislation on the Swedish or American lines about public access to official documents. 'This was an interesitng suggestion . . .' they said. But they put the temptation sternly behind them:

> '. . . we decided on reflection that it was not one that we should adopt. it seemed to us that this suggestion raised important constitutional questions going beyond our terms of reference' (para 85).

Since the Committee cannot be criticized for not doing something they were not asked—indeed not empowered—to do, their Report must be judged in the light of its restrictive terms of reference.

The Report did not have a good reception. The Government of the day thought it went too far; they accepted the principle that section 2 should be abolished and a new Act put in its place, but were apprehensive about the Committee's proposed categorization. The Report was debated in the House of Commons in June 1973 (H.C. Deb., 29 June 1973, vol. 858 c. 1885–1973), and the Home Secretary warned the House that he would probably have to widen the proposed area of criminal sanctions, on the familiar ground that one category of information merged imperceptibly into another, and that it was impossible to legislate for every eventuality. He also foresaw serious complications in determining who should do the classifying on the fringe of the reserved subjects, and how such classification could be challenged, except by calling on the courts to decide matters which were not within their proper competence. Hence the Government's preference for a theoretical but liberally interpreted embargo on all official information.

But if the Government and the civil service found the proposals too bold, writers in both newspapers and learned journals found them too timid. Some of the latter were elegantly dismissive, though perhaps more dogmatic than might have been expected in this quarter, since assertion was more prominent than argument. The newspapers were severe, and occasionally splenetic. The Report seemed to have few friends, but it is interesting to note that some years earlier the JUSTICE Working Party (p. 34) had arrived at much the same conclusions as Franks, save that they did not take into consideration Cabinet documents and Cabinet secrecy. The Official Secrets Acts were not of course the Working Party's only or main concern, as they were examining all aspects of the relationship between the law and the press, but in the short section devoted to government secrecy they wrote with balanced coolness, and would presumably have treated the Franks Report with more respect than its actual critics.

But whatever view is taken of the Franks recommendations it is common ground that they do nothing whatever to increase public access to official information. They will, if implemented, narrow the scope of the criminal law and will relieve the press of the anxiety and uncertainty that have hung over them in the past; though they have disappointed the press by not accepting a proposal frequently advanced in evidence on their behalf, namely that it should be a defence in a prosecution that publication was in the public interest. This was also the view—indeed it was the sole recommendation under this head—of the JUSTICE Working Party:

'We recommend that it should be a valid defence in any prosecution under the Official Secrets Act to show that the national interest or legitimate private interests confided to the State were not likely to be harmed and that the information was passed and received in good faith and in the public interest.'

The Franks Report – The Government's Statement of Intent

In November 1976 the Home Secretary, in making his statement of intent to the House of Commons (p. 11) spoke in very different accents from those of his predecessor in June 1973. Not only did the Government accept the Franks Committee's general approach but they proposed that in two respects its proposals should be 'liberalized'; it happened that the Home Secretary himself had been a member of the Franks Committee, but as he said 'Water has gone under the bridge . . .' since then. On the other hand there was one important respect in which the Government wished to be less liberal than Franks.

The first of the two proposed relaxations derived from the following statement of principle:

'. . . in considering the categories of information that ought to be protected by the criminal law we think it right to draw a clearer distinction between home and economic policy on the one hand and security and intelligence, defence and international relations on the other.'

from which the Government drew the moral that criminal sanctions should be removed from the Franks Committee's third category (currency and the reserves) *unless* the information was given or acquired for the purposes of private gain. The distinction between foreign and domestic financial affairs having become modified of recent years the only logical alternative would have been to extend the protection of the criminal law to home economic matters, and this was unacceptable.

The other proposed relaxation concerned Cabinet papers, over which the Franks proposals had thrown a comprehensive blanket, irrespective of their subject matter:

'The Government have concluded that Cabinet and Cabinet committee documents should be protected by criminal sanctions only when, by their content and security classification, they fall into one or other of the categories so protected.

These relaxations would be counter-balanced by an extension of the criminal law to an area where Franks had thought it inappropriate. The Franks proposal (see p. 73 *infra*) was that it should apply to defence matters which were classified 'Defence—Confidential' and which concerned military weapons and equipment. But:

'The Government have concluded that confidential information of a sensitive and potentially damaging kind goes rather wider than this in both the defence and international fields. It extends to certain areas of defence policy and strategy and of international relations where unauthorized disclosure would be prejudicial to British interests, to relations with a foreign government or to the safety of British citizens. The Government therefore propose to extend this Franks concept to become 'Defence and International—Confidential' and to define it somewhat more widely than Franks.'

This would be an important extension, especially perhaps in the matter of 'relations with a foreign government'. The *Sunday Telegraph* affair, for example, was clearly damaging to friendly relations with the Nigerian Government and would, if the Government's proposals had prevailed at the time, have come within the scope of the criminal law, instead of being used by the Court as an occasion to ridicule section 2.

The Home Secretary's statement took the House of Commons by surprise—one Member congratulated him on his own security arrangements—and several MPs asked why he had made it at all, and whether it ought not to have been the subject of a Green or White Paper instead of a short announcement. Mr. Rees explained that it was a long time since the Franks Committee had reported and that he owed the House an interim statement of intent. As to a Green Paper, he thought the Franks Report was 'green' enough.

We need something far 'whiter' on which people can think.

The Houghton Report on Cabinet Security

This Report (see p. 11) was published within almost a week of the
Government's statement of intent on open government, which seems to
have led the media to conclude that the statement was thereby modified
or had received a set-back. But the statement of intent was concerned
with what should and should not be secret, including what Cabinet
matters should and should not be secret; the Houghton Report with the
actual security of what *was* secret. It dealt with internal procedures for
keeping secrets secret and is not strictly relevant to the subject of
this essay.

CONCLUSION

Having said repeatedly in the course of this essay that official secrets were only incidental to the subject of open government, we ought now to turn from the Official Secrets Acts, which are its negative aspect, and consider its positive possibilities.

Here we encounter two connected difficulties. First, those who are strongest in their condemnation of official secrecy are least precise as to the kind of information which they think ought to be disclosed; second, only those who hold secret information know what it is, and are therefore in the privileged position of deciding what is good for people to know, which is precisely what infuriates those who do not know.

As to the first of these difficulties, it is perhaps natural that those who gave evidence to the Franks Committee, or who have since animadverted in the press, should have been moved by the exceptional rather than the ordinary—the cases where the Government is apparently being 'cagey' about something important, or where security, Crown privilege or a major planning decision is in issue. Less has been said publicly about the 99 per cent of official information which lacks publicity value but affects the day-to-day lives of ordinary people, information which is of course much more difficult for the public to identify or define. An interesting definition of the areas where it should be more readily accessible was made by Joseph Jacob, who suggested that the subjects which gave rise to pressure groups—for example housing, social security and the environment—are the ones where '. . . governmental secrecy is in part responsible for . . .' the discontent.[1] This is a helpful suggestion, and is a refreshing change from the customary concentration on scandals and *causes célèbres*, but in order to want information the public must know what information they want, and this would involve either an amendment of the law, going some way towards the American Freedom of Information Act, or, as the Franks Committee thought more to the point, an even more rapid and radical change in the mental attitude of civil servants towards this aspect of their work, achieving by administrative discretion and decision what is achieved in Sweden and the United States by statute.

This prompts the question why some countries seem to have no difficulty in implementing 'freedom of access' legislation, while in

---

[1] 'Some Reflections on Government Secrecy', *Public Law*, Spring 1974.

Britain the Government finds it impossibly difficult to contemplate. The Franks Committee based their own argument against such legislation on constitutional considerations, and principally on the view that it would not accord with the British principle of ministerial accountability and the anonymity of the civil service. But this ignores the fact that the principle no longer goes unchallenged. It was no ranting journalist but the sober Fulton Report which said that the assumption on which the doctrine rested was 'no longer tenable' (para. 283). 'The Minister and his junior ministers cannot know all that is going on in his department'—which is obvious—but moreover that 'the administration suffers from the convention that they do'. The same section of the Report went on to say, in effect, that since civil servants could not answer legitimate questions about departmental activities these questions went unanswered, and concluded:

> 'In our view, therefore, the concept of anonymity should be modified and civil servants, as professional administrators, should be able to go further than now in explaining what their departments are doing.'

There are two sides to the convention of anonymity. The one usually presented is that civil servants would not offer advice so freely and frankly if there were a danger that it could be disclosed, either to the public or to a successor Government. The more sinister side—so it is alleged—is that the convention allows mistakes or bad advice to be covered up, to the detriment of 'the public interest', an aspect of the subject which greatly appeals to commentators outside the civil service. Joseph Jacob, in the article quoted, couples the rise in pressure groups with the fall of interest in political parties, and attributes the current unpopularity of politicians to the fact that they consistently promise more than is fulfilled. But, he suggests, the failure to fulfil promises is not necessarily because it is impossible to fulfil them, but may be because 'the administrative machine lacks the skill or because of external factors over which they have no control.' Official secrecy covers all this up, and politicians take the blame.

A more forthright, and more recent, writer lists some of the more egregious *gaffes* committed by the British Government in recent years and asks why the public should not know who was responsible for the advice that lay behind them.[2] The prospect of civil servants' heads rolling is always an exhilarating one to those outside the service, but

[2] Anthony Harris, 'A Civil Servants' Magna Carta', *Financial Times*, 3 August 1976. Not that the writer is antagonistic to civil servants, for it is, according to him, 'Ministers who stuff idiotic measures from their manifesto down the throats of choking departments, knowing that the warnings of their officials will never reach the ears of the Opposition'.

once again the obsession with the exceptional does little to advance a rational discussion of open government. It is exceptional, not normal, for civil servants to make bad mistakes, and when they do so the internal discipline of their department, if they are culpable, or their failure to be promoted, if their judgement is bad, are surely sufficient without public retribution and obloquy.

The real point at issue is whether the pronouncements of Fulton and Franks are being taken seriously and whether the exhortations of ESTACODE (p. 33) are seriously meant. The 'liberalizing trends' described on page 18 are commendable, but it must be admitted that their pace is slow, since those brought up in the tradition of reticence do not find it palatable to adjust to openness. This is doubtless too dogmatic a statement, and is hardly susceptible of proof, but it does appear that the civil service *tradition* in Britain is stronger and more deep-rooted than in most countries, and secrecy a greater part of it. An interesting Commonwealth sidelight is given by an Australian scholar, writing of its transposition (which she regrets) to her own country, and tracing its roots to the days when civil servants were the king's own private servants, looking after his property and interests. The tradition of excessive secrecy can, she maintains, be ascribed to these origins. She goes on to point out that in the United States there is no evidence that the Freedom of Information Act has impeded the performance of public functions or diminished the quality of services provided, and suggests that this in in part because the civil service in the States is not an élite profession, with codes, conventions and a powerful *esprit de corps*, but merely a body of men hired to do a particular kind of job. They do not make a mystery of government.[3]

However, the question how quickly or how slowly the British civil service is adapting to more open government is—once again—obscured by the lure of the exceptional and the scandalous. It was the Secretary to the Cabinet who brought the wrath of the press upon his head and caused a public furore by saying that openness (in a particular matter) would 'hinder good government' or would 'not be in the public interest'. The phrases may not have been happily chosen, or he may have underrated the extent to which the general public is irritated by—as it seems to them—such a patronizing tone. Who is he to decide what is in the public's interest ? Have the public no view on this themselves ? But he was speaking of the quite unprecedented circumstance of a Cabinet Minister disclosing in precise detail what was said in Cabinet meetings, not of normal matters.

[3] 'Public Access to Government Documents', an unusually interesting article by Professor Enid Campbell in the *Australian Law Journal*, 1967, p. 73.

The awkward question none the less remains—who is to say what we ought to know, or what is fit for us to know? 'The public' can hardly decide for itself, which means, in the absence of legislation defining what we are entitled to know, that someone must decide for us. We live under a system of privilege, in which:

'all official information, whether or not related to national security, is the property of the Crown. It is therefore privileged and those who receive it may not divulge it without the Crown's authority.'[4]

But in matters of this kind, who is 'the Crown'?

Since the Franks Report attached so much importance to constitutional considerations it is natural to turn for enlightenment to the Royal Commission on the Constitution (Cmnd. 5460), which started work before the Franks Committee but reported a year later, and which at least showed itself aware that official secrecy was a problem. Unfortunately it offers only the most resounding of platitudes. Having admirably summed up the viewpoint of the critics it can do no better than this:

'While there is substance in these criticisms, we think that the expectations of some critics are probably unrealistic. The whole question of secrecy is bound up with delicate problems of diplomacy and practical administration which cannot simply be ignored in the interests of more open government.' (para. 320)

In their Memorandum of Dissent Lord Crowther-Hunt and Professor Peacock are a little more positive:

'To command the support of the people it is essential that the processes of government and decision making should be as open as possible. This is a vital characteristic of any democracy. If people do do not know what is going on they are not able to bring their influence to bear before final decisions are taken. The greater the secrecy, the greater the sense of exclusion from the decision making process and the greater the difficulty of gaining public acceptance for the decisions arrived at—and very probably, too, the worse the decisions. No doubt it will always be necessary to impose some limitations on the principle that in a democracy all decisions should be "open decisions openly arrived at"; but in a mature democracy those limitations must clearly be kept to an absolute minimum'.

Even so, they leave us where we started, so far as knowing what to do next is concerned.

However, it is one thing to complain that these eminent men were platitudinous, quite another to improve upon their platitudes. Neither

[4] 'Big Brother Knows Best', William Birtles, *Public Law*, 1973, p. 100.

the Franks Committee (regrettably) nor the Kilbrandon Commission (obviously) were applying their minds to the subject of open government, and what they had to say was incidental to their proper subjects. One can simply regret the fact that the Franks Committee was not given the terms of reference that Fulton had suggested.

The Franks Committee was of course skirting the subject throughout but was not commissioned and could not be expected to get to grips with it. In their own words:

> 'To the extent to which there is a connection between openness in government and the law relating to official information, our proposals to replace section 2 by much narrower provisions would represent a move towards greater openness'.

But this, good as far as it goes, is far removed from the positive requirements of the Swedish or American type of legislation.

To the average person this seems pre-eminently a subject where a middle way has got to be found. Where public affairs are concerned everyone is aggrieved by having to establish his 'need to know' instead of being able to feel that he has a right to know, and tends to be irritated by the sealed lips of those in authority. On the other hand everyone who has ever attempted to achieve anything, however modest, through the medium of a public body knows that without confidentiality the purposes of that body could not be achieved.

The choice seems to be between gradualism and legislation. The former has largely been the subject of this essay and its achievements should not be underrated. On the other hand gradualism in this matter has been *too* gradual for the temper of the times, especially when a succession of mildly scandalous events has stimulated public interest and whetted the reforming appetite. 'Open government', ill-defined though the expression may be, is a banner under which many are now prepared to march and there is probably no going back.

Whether we shall go forward to legislation rather than to administrative reform remains to be seen, though legislation would probably have to wait for several years. It is now probably too late for the proposed Public Information Bill, assuming that time is found for it in 1977–8, to go beyond the matters considered by Franks—that is the liberalizing of something that is restrictive and archaic—to introducing something new and positive which requires government to operate in a more open way. The Draft Bill of the parliamentary pressure group mentioned on page 58 (the All Party Committee for Freedom of Information) is ready and waiting, under the title of the Freedom of Information and Privacy Bill, and no doubt its sponsors will be active during the coming Session. It would indeed seem sensible that if ever we are to have legislation on the reform of the Official Secrets Act, on giving more generous access to official information and on protecting individual privacy we should do it all together.

On the other hand the fundamental requirement of open government, which is that ministers and civil servants should accept as a matter of course that they must give full reasons for their decisions and must provide all relevant information about policies and proposals, could surely be achieved—as so much has been achieved—by administrative decision and without the need to compel civil servants to disclose working documents and communications not intended for publication, with the further growth of bureaucracy and adjudication that this would entail. For it would be naïve to suppose that an Act of Parliament on Swedish or American lines could be implemented without large numbers of additional civil servants and a large invasion of the productive time of existing ones. The *cost* of open government has been its least discussed aspect.

Meanwhile, such is the pace of change of traditional concepts, it now appears that even devolution, remote though it may seem, could impinge upon our subject. According to *The Times* (16 November 1976):

> 'The possible status of Welsh assembly civil servants is likely to prove the most novel element of all from the point of view of British administrative practice. Although still United Kingdom officials, bound by the Civil Service Code of Conduct and the Official Secrets Act, they are more likely to assume the character of local government officials, speaking and being questioned in open committee session.
>
> The prospect of a British civil servant's having his policy advice made public and, very likely, repudiated in public as well, is without precedent in modern times. As they will serve both majority and minority members of committee, a more open system of government is assured.'

It could well be another step along the road.

Appendix

CLASSIFICATION PROCEDURES

The classification of official information is described in the written evidence of the Civil Service Department to the Franks Committee (Report Vol 2, pp. 15-23). The following description of the four categories (italicized) are quoted *verbatim*. The examples are taken from the same source, but are condensed for reasons of space.

(1) TOP SECRET

Information and material the unauthorized disclosure of which would *cause exceptionally grave damage to the nation.*

Examples would be largely drawn from the field of higher defence strategy and policy, but could also include plans which might endanger the stability of the currency or the reserves, or major plans of a political character; plans for the direct rule of Northern Ireland are cited as an example of the last category.

(2) SECRET

. . . cause serious injury to the interests of the nation.

Examples would be of the same general order, but would in the judgement of the person classifying them be somewhat less serious, being against the nation's interest rather than actual safety; they would include information whose disclosure would prejudice relations with friendly governments.

(3) CONFIDENTIAL

. . . be prejudicial to the interests of the nation.

For example, routine reports of a political, military or economic nature, economic forecasts on which future policy is based, planning and compulsory purchase, proposals to vary rates or duties.

(4) RESTRICTED

. . . be undesirable in the interests of the nation.

For example, routine military documents, departmental instructions, draft Bills.

The examples, which are highly condensed, do not purport to do more than convey the flavour of the kinds of information thus graded. They are possibly sufficient, however, to make clear that one classification merges into another, and that sharp definitions are difficult. Since it follows that there is a fairly large subjective element in deciding the appropriate category, it should be mentioned that the person deciding the classification is the originator of the document. He is given elaborate guidelines ('Aids to correct Classification and Regrading') which lay particular stress on the undesirability of 'over-grading', for reasons both of principle—since over-grading 'debases the currency'—and of expediency—since the cost of making Top Secret and Secret documents secure is considerable. Instructions are also given with regard to regular periodic reviews of classification, for the purpose of down-grading or destruction.

Top Secret information apart, the test for classification is whether, in varying degrees, the 'interests of the nation' would be adversely affected. But in this area of the subject, as in others, the Government must also have regard to the interests of those who have entrusted them with confidential information, whether they be commercial firms or private individuals. As we have seen, the departments dealing with income tax, customs and excise, industry and trade and the social services are notable recipients of such information. It is not classified, but is accorded a 'privacy marking', consisting of the phrase 'In Confidence' preceded by the subject matter, e.g. 'Commercial—In Confidence'.

The Franks Proposals

As matters stand classification has no connection with the criminal law, i.e. a prosecution under the Official Secrets Act is unrelated to the degree of classification of the information alleged to have been disclosed. Classification is a purely administrative device, governed by internal civil service instructions. The Franks Committee sought to identify the kinds of information that required the protection of criminal sanctions, and to distinguish them from the rest, by attaching a specific classification to each item. The information in question, as we said on page 59, comprised defence and internal security, foreign relations, the currency and the reserves; as to its classification, it was thought unnecessary to revise the present *nomenclature*, but to impose criminal sanctions only if the classification contained the word SECRET, or in the case of military matters DEFENCE—CONFIDENTIAL.

It was recommended that the Secretary of State should make statutory regulations about classification and declassification of documents, which should include provisions on levels of authority at which decisions on classification may be taken and on arrangements for review and declassification.

Before a decision was taken to prosecute the Minister personally should consider whether, *at the time of the alleged disclosure*, the information had been properly classified.

An interesting addition to these technical recommendations, and one of particular importance to the subject of this essay, was to the effect that the Prime Minister should appoint an informal, non-statutory Committee, whose purpose would be to overcome both the ignorance of the facts about classification and suspicion of its motives on the part of those affected by it (representatives of the news media and any other interests directly affected). It was thought that by such means the Government could offer not only explanations but co-operation, e.g. through consultation on the proposed regulations or advice as to whether information which had come into the hands of the press was classified or not.

Nationalized Industries

The nationalized industries do not have any agreed or standardized system of classification. For Government information the Government's own classification would normally be followed (e.g. Government Secret, Government Confidential etc.) and the Official Secrets Acts would apply, but the protection of confidential information originating in the industry itself would be a matter for internal procedures and disciplines and could well vary from one industry to another (the Post Office and the Atomic Energy Authority excepted). It is possible for difficulties to arise in the 'grey' area between the two, as when information

73

originating in an industry is later incorporated in a Government document and given a classification; or it may not always be made known to an industry when Government information has been de-classified. Otherwise, classification does not appear to have given rise to trouble.

Local Government

The position in local government is ill-defined. Standing Orders have no legal force, and may depart considerably in the direction of openness on the one hand or secrecy on the other from the Model Order recommended by the Department. The matter is complicated by the fact that while members of a local authority staff are subject to internal discipline if they wilfully or indiscreetly disclose information which they know to be confidential, no such sanctions can be applied to *members* of the authority (i.e. the elected councillors). The marking of documents 'Confidential' is a restraining influence but could hardly prevent a councillor from disclosing the contents if he were determined to do so, and he would suffer no penalty.

However, this has not emerged as a serious problem in local government, whose record has been consistently excellent. It has been marred in recent years by the somewhat different phenomenon of *corruption*, whereby members or senior officers have profited financially from their knowledge or position or have accepted bribes. But these have been isolated *causes célèbres*, and happily appear to be rare exceptions to the general rule.

THE CONSUMER CAUSE

A Short Account of its Organization Development, Power and Importance

RONALD WRAITH

' . . . Mr. Wraith has performed a useful service in producing what could well turn out to be the standard work on this subject . . . one which should find its way on to the book-shelves of all those concerned with consumer affairs. It is unlikely to remain there passively since it is sure to be frequently consulted.' *Public Administration.*

'The book is recommended as essential background reading for new entrants to the profession and, in particular, to students taking the D.C.A. course.' The *Monthly Review*, Institute of Trading Standards Administration.

1976   £1.50   (£1.20 to members)

APPRAISAL FOR STAFF DEVELOPMENT

A Public Sector Study

RONALD WRAITH

'This should be required reading, not just for anyone professionally or personally interested in staff development, but also for the zealots whose passion for completeness threatens at times to submerge their industries in full frontal "MBO" whether they were suited to it or not.' *Public Administration*

'The book is written in admirably clear and simple English and is commended to anyone who wishes to keep abreast of current thinking in this field.'

Edgar Anstey, *London Review of Public Administration*

1975   £1.80   (£1.40 to members)

RIPA BOOKLETS

FINANCING PUBLIC SECTOR PENSIONS

RAYMOND NOTTAGE

'Mr. Nottage's research provides a new light on a subject which is gaining importance in these inflationary times. The pension funds are rapidly growing financial giants demanding ever greater sums of money from the public, both the private and public sector. No one has asked them why they are demanding this money when they cannot even spend most of what they have.' Richard Redden in the *Guardian*.

'What Raymond Nottage has made penetratingly clear, and in a succinct fashion, is that today's jumble of public pension schemes needs revision on more logical lines. Harold B. Rose in *Public Administration*.

1975   £1.00   (75p to members)

THE MAJOR PUBLIC CORPORATIONS: A STATUTORY ANALYSIS

DAVID PEIRSON

A comparative analysis by a former Secretary to the U.K. Atomic Energy Authority of the key statutes governing the major public corporations in the United Kingdom.

'. . . a very useful reference booklet, the information in which would require a considerable amount of research to extract from the statutes constituting these corporations.' *Rating and Valuation*.

'It is brief and clear and uninvolved—and well worth one pound.' *Journal of Administration Overseas*.

1974   £1.00   (75p to members)